MILITARY AND VETERAN ISSUES

VETERANS' ACCESS TO MENTAL HEALTH CARE

ASSESSMENTS

MILITARY AND VETERAN ISSUES

Additional books in this series can be found on Nova's website under the Series tab.

Additional e-books in this series can be found on Nova's website under the eBooks tab.

MILITARY AND VETERAN ISSUES

VETERANS' ACCESS TO MENTAL HEALTH CARE

ASSESSMENTS

EDGAR W. SCHNEIDER
EDITOR

nova publishers
New York

Library of Congress Cataloging-in-Publication Data

ISBN: 978-1-63485-195-4

Published by Nova Science Publishers, Inc. † New York

Contents

PREFACE

Between 2005 and 2013, the number of veterans receiving mental health care from the Department of Veterans Affairs' (VA) Veterans Health Administration (VHA) increased 63 percent, outpacing overall growth in veterans receiving any VHA health care. In fiscal year 2014, VHA spent more than $3.9 billion providing outpatient specialty mental health care (mental health care) to more than 1.5 million veterans. This book examines, among other things, veterans' access to timely mental health care, and VHA's related oversight.

In: Veterans' Access to Mental Health Care ISBN: 978-1-63485-195-4
Editor: Edgar W. Schneider

Chapter 1

VA MENTAL HEALTH: CLEARER GUIDANCE ON ACCESS POLICIES AND WAIT-TIME DATA NEEDED*

United States Government Accountability Office

WHY GAO DID THIS STUDY

Between 2005 and 2013, the number of veterans receiving mental health care from VHA increased 63 percent, outpacing overall growth in veterans receiving any VHA health care. In fiscal year 2014, VHA spent more than $3.9 billion providing outpatient specialty mental health care (mental health care) to more than 1.5 million veterans.

GAO was asked to examine VHA's efforts to provide timely access to mental health care for veterans. This report examines, among other things, (1) veterans' access to timely mental health care, and (2) VHA's related oversight. GAO conducted site visits to five VAMCs selected to provide variation in factors such as location and mental health care utilization rates; reviewed a randomly selected, nongeneralizable sample of 100 medical records (20 from each of the five selected VAMCs) for veterans new to mental health care who received treatment between July 1, 2014, and September 30, 2014; and interviewed VHA and VAMC officials on VHA's measures and oversight of

* This is an edited, reformatted and augmented version of a United States Government Accountability Office, Publication No. GAO-16-24, dated October 2015.

access to mental health care. GAO evaluated VHA's oversight of access to mental health care against relevant federal standards for internal control.

WHAT GAO RECOMMENDS

GAO recommends that VHA issue clarifying guidance on (1) access policies; (2) definitions used to calculate wait times; and (3) how open-access appointments are to be managed. VHA concurred with GAO's recommendations but disagreed with certain of its findings, for example, GAO's calculation of overall wait-times. GAO maintains its findings, as discussed in the report, are valid.

WHAT GAO FOUND

The way in which the Department of Veterans Affairs' (VA) Veterans Health Administration (VHA) calculates veteran mental health wait times may not always reflect the overall amount of time a veteran waits for care. VHA uses a veteran's preferred date (determined when an appointment is scheduled) to calculate the wait time for that patient's full mental health evaluation, the primary entry point for mental health care. Of the 100 veterans whose records GAO reviewed, 86 received full mental health evaluations within 30 days of their preferred dates. On average, this was within 4 days. However, GAO also found

- veterans' preferred dates were, on average, 26 days after their initial requests or referrals for mental health care, and ranged from 0 to 279 days. Further, GAO found the average time in which veterans received their first treatment across the five VA medical centers (VAMC) in its review ranged from 1 to 57 days from the full mental health evaluation.
- conflicting access policies for allowable wait times for a full mental health evaluation—14 days (according to VHA's mental health handbook) versus 30 days (set in response to recent legislation) from the veteran's preferred date—created confusion among VAMC officials about which policy they are expected to follow. These conflicting policies are inconsistent with federal internal control

standards and can hinder officials' ability to ensure veterans are receiving timely access to mental health care.

VHA monitors access to mental health care, but the lack of clear policies on wait-time data precludes effective oversight. GAO found VHA's wait-time data may not be comparable over time and between VAMCs. Specifically

- data may not be comparable over time. VHA has not clearly communicated the definitions used, such as how a new patient is identified, or changes made to these definitions. This limits the reliability and usefulness of the data in determining progress in meeting stated objectives for veterans' timely access to mental health care.
- data may not be comparable between VAMCs. For example, when open-access appointments are used, data are not comparable between VAMCs. Open-access appointments are typically blocks of time for veterans to see providers without a scheduled appointment. GAO found inconsistencies in the implementation of these appointments, including one VAMC that manually maintained a list of veterans seeking mental health care outside of VHA's scheduling system. Without guidance stating how to manage and track open-access appointments, data comparisons between VAMCs may be misleading. Moreover, VAMCs may lose track of patients referred for mental health care, placing veterans at risk for negative outcomes.

Abbreviations

CBOC	community-based outpatient clinic
CMHC	community mental health clinics
HHS	Department of Health and Human Services
OIG	Office of Inspector General
PC3	Patient-Centered Community Care
PTSD	post-traumatic stress disorder
SAIL	Strategic Analytics for Improvement and Learning
VA	Department of Veterans Affairs
VAMC	Veterans Affairs Medical Center
VCP	Veterans Choice Program
Choice Act	Veterans Access, Choice, and Accountability Act of 2014

VHA	Veterans Health Administration
VISN	Veterans Integrated Service Network
VistA	Veterans Health Information Systems and Technology Architecture

* * *

October 28, 2015

The Honorable Johnny Isakson
Chairman
Committee on Veterans' Affairs
United States Senate

The Honorable Jeff Miller
Chairman
Committee on Veterans' Affairs
House of Representatives

The Honorable Richard Burr
United States Senate

The Honorable Joni K. Ernst
United States Senate

The Veterans Health Administration (VHA), within the Department of Veterans Affairs (VA), has seen a significant increase in demand for mental health services. Between 2005 and 2013, the number of veterans who received mental health care from VHA increased 63 percent, more than 3 times the rate of increase seen in the overall number of veterans using any VHA health care services. VHA reported a significant portion of this increase was due to an influx of veterans returning from the conflicts in Iraq and Afghanistan, and to its proactive screening to identify veterans with symptoms that may be associated with depression, post-traumatic stress disorder (PTSD), substance abuse disorder, or who may have experienced military sexual trauma.

In fiscal year 2014, VHA estimated that more than 1.5 million veterans obtained outpatient mental health care for conditions such as PTSD, depression, and substance abuse.[1] VHA provides mental health care in its more than 1,200 facilities in both specialty settings—those that primarily provide mental health care—and in other settings, such as primary care. Additionally, VHA may pay for mental health care provided by non-VA providers in the community. In fiscal year 2014, VHA spent more than $3.9 billion providing outpatient specialty mental health care in its facilities, and more than $34 million for outpatient specialty mental health care provided by non-VA providers.[2]

In recent years, we and others have expressed concerns about veterans' ability to access timely mental health care, and VHA's oversight of patient scheduling practices.[3] For example, we previously identified the reliability of reported wait times and patient scheduling oversight as areas for improvement.[4] Also, in 2012, the VA Office of Inspector General (OIG) reported that VHA was not consistently providing new veterans with timely access to comprehensive mental health evaluations, and had overstated its success in providing veterans with timely new and follow-up appointments for mental health treatment. An August 2012 Executive Order directed VHA to improve mental health access by, among other things, hiring additional staff and gauging the effectiveness of the use of community-based providers by establishing a community provider pilot program.[5] In addition, the Veterans Access, Choice, and Accountability Act of 2014 (Choice Act), enacted in August 2014, provided additional non-VA care options for veterans facing long waits or lengthy travel distances to obtain VHA health care services.[6]

You asked us to examine issues related to VHA's efforts to provide timely access to mental health care for veterans. This report examines

1) veterans' access to timely mental health care,
2) VHA's oversight of timely access to mental health care,
3) VHA's hiring of mental health staff since 2012 and the effects, if any, of that hiring on access to mental health care, and
4) VHA's community provider pilot program's effects, if any, on veterans' access to mental health care.

We limited our scope to outpatient specialty mental health care, which we refer to as mental health care for the purposes of this report, because the majority of veterans with either a possible or a confirmed mental illness, about 70 percent and 85 percent respectively, are treated by VHA through outpatient mental health.[7] To address all four objectives, we conducted site visits to five VA medical centers (VAMC): Atlanta VAMC (Decatur, Georgia); George H. O'Brien, Jr. VAMC (Big Spring, Texas); Hunter Holmes McGuire VAMC (Richmond, Virginia); Portland VAMC (Portland, Oregon); and Sioux Falls

VA Health Care System (Sioux Falls, South Dakota).[8] These VAMCs were selected for variation in facility complexity level, geographic location, mental health care utilization, mental health appointment wait times, the number of mental health staff hired since 2012, and participation in the community provider pilot program.[9] At each site, we visited the VAMC as well as one affiliated community-based outpatient clinic (CBOC) that provided mental health care.[10] Additionally, at the two sites that participated in the community provider pilot program, we visited two of the community-based providers that participated in the program. The results from our five VAMC visits cannot be generalized to all VHA facilities.

To examine veterans' ability to access timely mental health care and VHA's oversight of this access, we reviewed relevant VHA and VAMC documents, and interviewed staff from VHA's central office, the five selected VAMCs, and the five Veterans Integrated Service Networks (VISN) that oversee the selected VAMCs about the current policies and guidance for scheduling mental health appointments.[11] We also interviewed stakeholders from other key organizations, such as Vet Centers and veteran service organizations, to gain their perspectives on mental health care access.[12] Further, for each of the five VAMCs we visited, we reviewed a randomly selected sample of medical records to assess the timeliness in which veterans received mental health appointments.[13] Our sample included 100 new veteran records, 20 for each VAMC, generally composed of 10 records for veterans who had a diagnosis of PTSD and 10 records for veterans who had any other (i.e., non-PTSD) mental health diagnoses. We considered veterans with PTSD separately because PTSD is considered one of the signature injuries of the conflicts in Iraq and Afghanistan. For new veterans, we examined the timeliness in which they received comprehensive mental health evaluations and follow-up mental health appointments as defined in VHA's policies, and, for new veterans with PTSD, we evaluated whether or not they were referred to, and completed, evidence-based therapies for PTSD—treatments specified by VHA as shown to be effective—in accordance with VHA's policies.[14] Four of the five VAMCs we visited offered inpatient mental health care. For those four VAMCs, we also reviewed 20 records, 5 from each VAMC, of recently discharged inpatients to assess the timeliness of their first follow-up mental health appointments following discharge.[15] Additionally, we reviewed a random sample of 15 records from a list one of the VAMCs we visited used to track veterans outside of VHA's scheduling system.[16] We reviewed these records to see whether the veterans received mental health care. Due to the small sample size of our medical record reviews, the results cannot be generalized across any single VHA facility or to all VHA facilities. Lastly, we evaluated VHA information on veteran wait times for mental health appointments and VHA's oversight of access to mental health care against the federal internal control standards related to control activities, information, and monitoring.[17]

To examine VHA's hiring of mental health staff since 2012 (the year of the relevant Executive Order) and any effects on access to mental health care, we analyzed national VHA mental health workforce data from fiscal year 2010 through fiscal year 2014, as well as the number of full-time-equivalent staff providing outpatient mental health care, before and after the hiring initiative. We also analyzed VHA data on hires by position type to determine the number and types of mental health staff hired as a result of the hiring initiative. Additionally, we reviewed vacancy rate data for mental health staff at each of the five VAMCs we visited and across VHA as of March 2015. We reviewed relevant VHA and VAMC documentation related to staffing and hiring initiatives and interviewed VHA, VISN, and VAMC officials about recruitment, hiring, and retention of outpatient specialty mental health staff, any effects these initiatives had on access to care, and the challenges to hiring or placing new staff. To determine the reliability of the workforce and vacancy data, we reviewed related documentation; performed manual and electronic tests of the data to identify any outliers or anomalies; and followed up with officials as necessary, incorporating the corrections we received. We determined that the data were sufficiently reliable for the purposes of our review. Finally, we reviewed a random, nongeneralizable sample of 30 records from VAMC transfer lists—15 from each of the two VAMCs we visited that were using them—that track veterans waiting for mental health care appointments at preferred locations.[18] We reviewed the records to identify whether these veterans were receiving care while waiting to be transferred to their preferred locations.

To examine the community provider pilot program's effects, if any, on veterans' access to mental health care, we reviewed relevant VHA documents related to the pilot program and other non-VA care programs and interviewed VHA, VISN, and VAMC staff on the use of these programs. We also collected information from the 10 VAMCs that referred veterans to community provider pilot sites to assess the extent to which VHA has referred veterans to these providers, and reviewed VHA's pilot program evaluation and related veteran satisfaction survey results.

We conducted this performance audit from September 2014 to October 2015 in accordance with generally accepted government auditing standards.

Those standards require that we plan and perform the audit to obtain sufficient, appropriate evidence to provide a reasonable basis for our findings and conclusions based on our audit objectives. We believe that the evidence obtained provides a reasonable basis for our findings and conclusions based on our audit objectives.

BACKGROUND

VHA provides a range of treatments and services to improve the mental health of veterans, including teaching coping skills and offering tailored programs to treat specific problems, such as depression, PTSD, and substance abuse disorders, and to promote recovery.[19] When needed mental health care is not available through a local VHA provider, VHA has avenues by which veterans may obtain care from non-VA providers in the community.

Veterans' Access to Mental Health Care

VHA policy states that veterans are entitled to timely access to mental health care. There are a number of ways a veteran may seek access to mental health care. (See fig. 1.) Upon initial referral or request for mental health care, veterans new to mental health care (those not seen by a mental health provider within the past 24 months through VHA) are to receive initial assessments from either referring providers (such as primary care physicians) or mental health providers; these assessments identify those who need urgent or immediate access to mental health care.[20] Following the initial assessment, a veteran is to receive timely access to a comprehensive mental health evaluation that includes a diagnosis and a plan for treatment. The comprehensive evaluation— referred to as a full mental health evaluation— serves as a veteran's main entry point to mental health care.

Additionally, established veterans (those who already have received mental health care within the past 24 months through VHA) are to receive timely access to follow-up care. Follow-up care may be provided by a single provider or, for those veterans who need a range of services, by multiple providers. For example, a veteran may receive ongoing care from both a psychiatrist and a psychologist to manage their symptoms. Veterans with specific diagnoses, such as PTSD, are to be considered for evidence-based therapies, such as cognitive processing therapy or prolonged exposure therapy, as clinically appropriate.[21] Furthermore, veterans discharged from inpatient mental health stays are to receive timely access to follow-up outpatient mental health care.

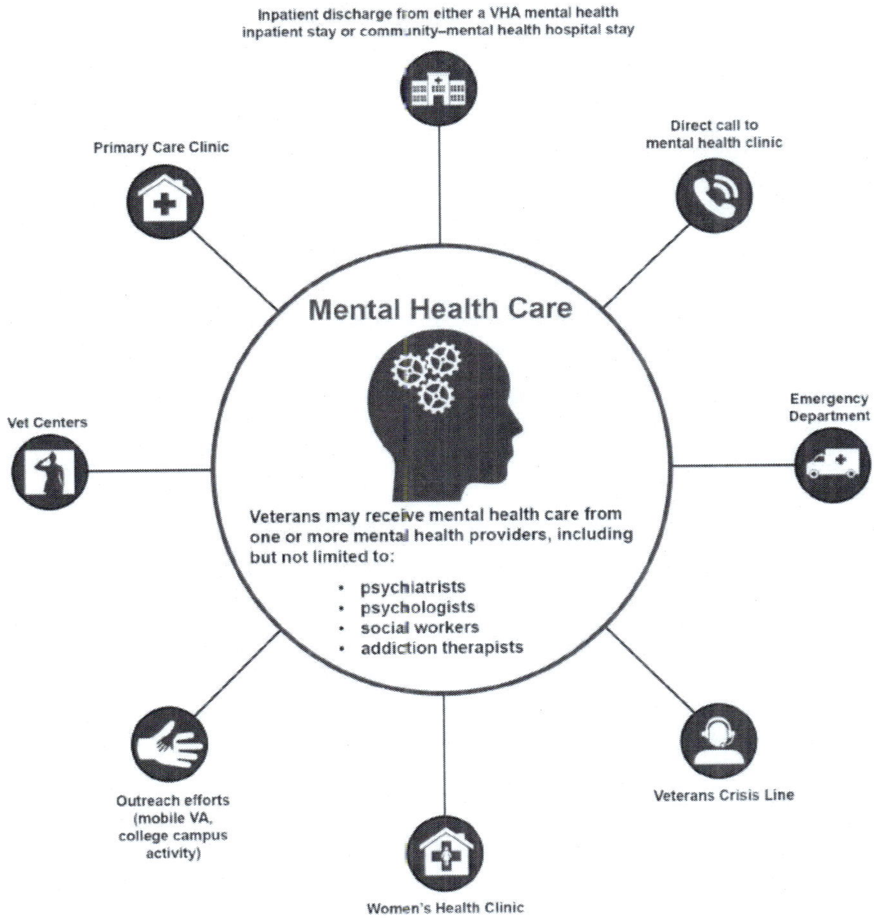

Source: VHA (information) and GAO (illustration). | GAO-16-24.

Figure 1. Common Pathways through Which Veterans Can Access Mental Health Care within the Veterans Health Administration (VHA).

VHA's scheduling policy establishes processes and procedures for scheduling medical appointments, including mental health appointments.[22] This policy requires schedulers to obtain and correctly record the preferred date—the date on which the veteran wants to be seen—in VHA's Veterans Health Information Systems and Technology Architecture (VistA).[23] VistA's scheduling component was implemented in 1985 and VA is considering several options for updating or replacing this scheduling component.

VHA Wait Time and Performance Data

In 1995, VHA established a policy of scheduling specialty care appointments, including mental health appointments, within 30 days of the date the veteran would like to be seen. In fiscal year 2011, based on reported improved performance, VHA shortened its wait-time policy to 14 days for new veterans. In fiscal year 2015, VHA set a new policy for new veterans in response to the Choice Act that veterans should be seen within 30 days of the date the veteran wants to be seen.[24] Currently, VHA also has a policy of providing outpatient mental health care to a veteran discharged from an inpatient mental health stay within 7 days and for providing follow-up care to an established veteran within 30 days of the clinically indicated date, commonly referred to as the return-to-clinic date.

To facilitate accountability for achieving its wait-time policies, VHA includes wait-time and other performance data, such as the "missed opportunity" rate—the percentage of scheduled appointments that were not used because veterans did not show up for their appointments—in several internal and external reports. VHA also makes publicly available on its website its patient access reports (including monthly average wait times for completed and pending mental health appointments for each VAMC), and its Strategic Analytics for Improvement and Learning (SAIL) reports, which assess VAMC performance across 25 quality measures, including death and medical complication rates, customer satisfaction, and access (based on wait-time data).

VHA Mental Health Providers

To meet the needs of veterans seeking mental health care, VHA has sought to increase its mental health staff, including the number of psychiatrists, psychologists, social workers, peer specialists and other mental health professionals.[25] In 2012, VHA began a two-part hiring initiative: (1) VHA's recruitment effort focused on hiring 1,600 new mental health professionals, 300 new non-clinical support staff and filling existing vacancies starting in June 2012; and (2) Executive Order 13265, issued in August 2012, authorized the hiring of 800 peer specialist positions by December 31, 2013, along with reiterating VHA's goal of hiring 1,600 new mental health professionals by June 30, 2013.

Non-VA Medical Care

Generally, eligible veterans may utilize the Non-VA Medical Care Program when a VAMC is unable to provide certain specialty care services, or when the veteran would have to travel long distances to obtain care at a VAMC. Non-VA providers generally treat veterans in non-VA facilities, such as physicians' offices or hospitals in the community, and are commonly paid by VHA using a fee-for-service arrangement.

There are several ways veterans can obtain care from non-VA providers.[26] For example, the August 2012 Executive Order required VHA to establish partnerships with community-based providers, such as community mental health clinics (CMHCs), under a pilot program, to help meet veterans' mental health needs in a timely manner. The goal for the pilot program was to decrease wait times and increase the geographic reach of VHA mental health services. The Executive Order required VHA to establish at least 15 pilot sites by February 27, 2013. In addition, in 2013, VA established the Patient Centered Community Care (PC3) program to deliver care to veterans when local VAMCs and CBOCs cannot provide the care due to demand exceeding capacity, geographic inaccessibility, or other factors.[27] More recently, the Choice Act authorized non-VA care, including mental health care, for veterans with certain access challenges. Under this authority, VHA created the Veterans Choice Program (VCP) with the goal of meeting demand for health care in the short term. Beginning in November 2014, for example, certain veterans were able to receive non-VA care if the next available medical appointment with a VA provider was more than 30 days from their preferred date or if they lived more than 40 miles from the nearest VA facility.[28] Recently passed legislation requires VHA to submit a plan to Congress by November 1, 2015 for consolidating its Non-VA Medical Care programs under a single program.[29]

MOST VETERANS IN OUR REVIEW RECEIVED CARE WITHIN 30 DAYS OF THEIR PREFERRED DATES, BUT VHA'S METHOD OF CALCULATING WAIT TIMES DOES NOT ALWAYS REFLECT OVERALL WAIT TIMES

Most Veterans Received Full Mental Health Evaluations within 30 Days of Their Preferred Dates, though VHA's Access Policies Conflict

Most veterans included in our review received full mental health evaluations, which provide new veterans with an entry point to access mental health care, in an average of 4 days of their preferred dates. At the five VAMCs we visited, the average time in which a veteran received this full evaluation ranged from 0 to 9 days from the preferred date. (See table 1.)

Table 1. Time Frames for which Veterans Received Full Mental Health Evaluations for Selected Veterans Affairs Medical Centers (VAMC)

VAMC	Average number of days from preferred date to full evaluation	Number of veterans seen within 14 days of preferred date	Number of veterans seen within 30 days of preferred date
A	0	20	20
B	0	16	16
C	9	16	18
D	7	14	16
E	3	15	16

Source: GAO analysis of Veterans Health Administration data. | GAO-16-24

Note: We reviewed 100 medical records (20 from each VAMC we visited) to determine how much time elapsed between a veteran's preferred date and the date of their full mental health evaluation.

VHA has two policies that conflict in their definitions of timely access to a full mental health evaluation for a veteran new to VHA mental health care: (1) a 14-day policy established by VHA's *Uniform Handbook for Mental Health Services*,[30] and (2) a 30-day policy set by VHA in response to the Choice Act.[31] To date, VHA has not provided guidance on which policy should be followed, which is inconsistent with federal internal control standards that call for management to clearly document, through management directives or administrative policies, significant events or activities, such as ensuring timely access to mental health care, to help ensure management directives are carried out properly.[32] VHA officials told us they are aware of the discrepancy and that there is an internal group working to revise the access policies for mental health care, as well as the *Uniform Handbook*, to ensure consistency, but the officials could not provide a timeline for completion. When we assessed the veteran records included in our sample against these two policies, we found that, across all five VAMCs, 86 of the 100 veterans included in our review received a full mental health evaluation within 30 days of the preferred date and 81 veterans received this evaluation within 14 days. As a result of the conflicting policies, a number of VHA officials, including VISN and VAMC officials, told us they do not know which policy they are currently expected to meet, which may make it difficult for them to ensure timely access in light of increasing demand for mental health care. By not clarifying which access policy currently applies to mental health care, VHA is limited in its ability to effectively manage timely access to mental health care.

VHA's Method of Calculating Wait Times Does Not Always Reflect Veterans' Overall Wait Times for Appointments and Services

Although the averages for the time between veterans' preferred dates and their full mental health evaluations were generally within several days, they may not reflect overall wait times. We found that because VHA uses veterans' preferred appointment date—not the date veterans initially request or are referred for mental health care—as the basis for its wait-time calculations, these calculations may only reflect a portion of veterans' overall wait time. This occurs because veterans generally are not asked for their preferred dates until some period of time after they request or are referred for mental health care.[33] (See fig. 2.)

On average, our review of 100 new veteran records found that a veteran's preferred date was 26 days after their initial request or referral for mental health care, though this varied by VAMC.[34] (See table 2.)

Delays between initial request or referral date and a veteran's preferred date may be due to a veteran not wanting to start treatment immediately. However, based on our review of records, we also found that some patients were delayed in receiving care because a facility did not adequately handle a referral to mental health care.

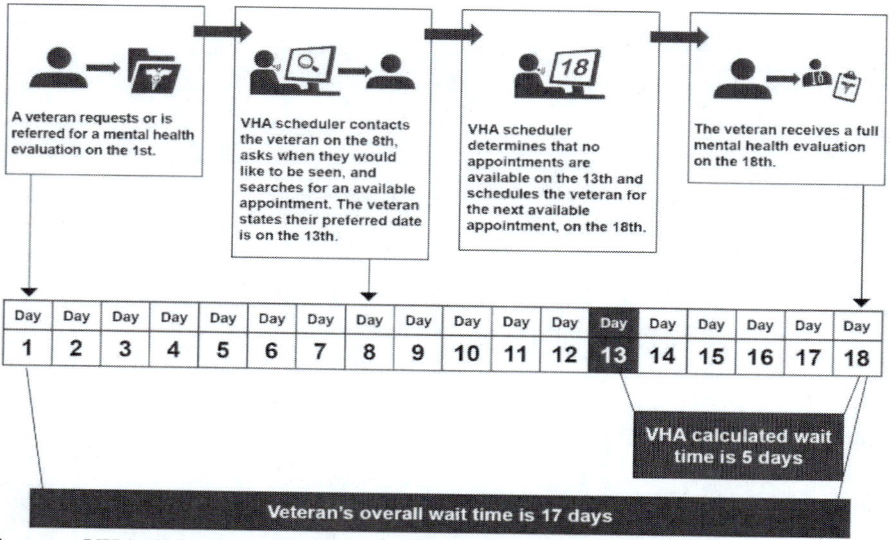

Sources: VHA (information) and GAO (illustration). | GAO-16-24.

Figure 2. Illustration of How Overall Wait Time May Differ from Veterans Health Administration's (VHA) Calculated Wait Time.

Table 2. Time Frames between Initial Date of Request or Referral for Mental Health Care and Veterans' Preferred Dates, by Selected Veterans Affairs Medical Centers (VAMC)

VAMC	Average number of days	Minimum number of days	Maximum number of days
A	28	0	104
B	41	0	279
C	15	0	57
D	27	0	181
E	18	0	74

Source: GAO analysis of Veterans Health Administration data. | GAO-16-24.

- For example, one veteran received a referral to psychology in November 2013 when the referring provider noted that the veteran should be evaluated for PTSD. However, no contact was made with the veteran until the veteran called back in July 2014 and asked for an evaluation. As a result, the veteran's preferred date was 279 days after the initial referral.

- Another referral led to a veteran waiting 174 days between their initial referral for mental health care and their preferred date. The veteran's primary care provider was supposed to have placed a referral to psychology in March 2014, but we could not find evidence of the referral ever being placed. Despite not placing a proper referral, the veteran's primary care provider alerted a VHA psychologist who reached out to the patient in March 2014, by phone, but did not leave a message. No VAMC mental health provider reached out again until September 2014, after the veteran's primary care provider made a referral (this time documented correctly). The veteran was then able to schedule a full mental health evaluation approximately 1 week later.
- One veteran called the suicide prevention hotline in August 2014 expressing suicidal thoughts and then hung up. The hotline staff contacted the VAMC and the local authorities who found the veteran intoxicated and took him to a local jail to stabilize. The VAMC contacted the veteran a couple days later to discuss mental health treatment (which the veteran declined at the time) but did not follow up again with the veteran until February 2015, when the veteran contacted a VHA social worker to say he was suffering from severe depression and continued to have suicidal thoughts. As a result, the veteran's preferred date was 181 days after the initial contact for mental health care.

Veterans who receive a full mental health evaluation may experience additional delays in receiving treatment. Our review found that veterans do not always begin treatment specific to their mental health condition (such as a prescription for medication or a course of psychotherapy) at the appointment in which they receive their first full mental health evaluation. We found this for 50 of the 100 new veterans whose records we reviewed.

- One veteran called into a VAMC expressing suicidal thoughts and was seen the same day for a full mental health evaluation, but no appointment for treatment was made at that time as the veteran was starting a new job. The veteran did not receive treatment for more than 7 months and the mental health providers at the facility did not document any attempts to contact the veteran during that time.[35]
- Two veterans with PTSD, both initially referred in March 2014, received their full mental health evaluations in April 2014, within 30 days of their initial requests or referrals. However, neither received

treatment until August 2014, nearly 4 months after their full mental health evaluations.

- Another veteran was initially referred to mental health care in September 2014 after a screening for veterans returning from the recent conflicts in Iraq and Afghanistan. While the veteran was seen for a full mental health evaluation within 30 days and subsequently seen in a PTSD orientation group, the veteran did not receive treatment until December 2014, nearly 80 days from the time of the full mental health evaluation. The veteran's file provided no indication of the reason for the treatment delay.

Based on our records review, we found that whether veterans received treatment for their mental health conditions during their full evaluation appointments was generally dependent on the type of mental health professional who conducted the evaluation. Generally speaking, veterans who were evaluated by a psychiatrist received some type of mental health treatment during their full evaluation appointments, while veterans who were evaluated by a psychologist or substance abuse professional often did not receive treatment specific to their mental health condition at their full evaluation appointments. We found that the timeliness in which veterans received this first treatment varied by VAMC included in our review. (See table 3.)

Table 3. Average Number of Days from Full Evaluation to First Treatment, by Selected Veterans Affairs Medical Centers (VAMC)

VAMC	Average number of days	Minimum number of days	Maximum number of days
A	20	0	77
B	57	0	218
C	4	0	53
D	10	0	70
E	1	0	14

Source: GAO analysis of Veterans Health Administration data. | GAO-16-24

The differences between the date of the initial request or referral to care and the preferred date are consistent with previous findings by the VA OIG, which found in 2012 that VHA's starting point for its wait-time calculation was not a meaningful measurement of a veteran's waiting time to receive an evaluation.[36] VHA officials agreed that the current calculation does not capture the time between when a veteran is referred to or requests mental health care and when the veteran is contacted to schedule a mental health appointment or to when a particular course of treatment starts, but also said there is currently no consensus on the appropriate standard or measure for when the calculation should begin or end.

VHA Is Generally Meeting Access Policies for Other Types of Mental Health Appointments

VHA's *Uniform Handbook* also defines policies for timely access to other types of mental health appointments, such as follow-up appointments and outpatient appointments following discharge from an inpatient mental health stay.[37] In particular,

- established veterans should receive follow-up appointments within 30 days of their return-to-clinic dates;
- veterans recently discharged from inpatient mental health stays should receive outpatient appointments (either by phone or in-person) within 7 days of discharge; and
- veterans with PTSD should receive evidence-based therapies for PTSD.

Our review found that veterans generally received follow-up appointments and post-discharge appointments in accordance with the *Uniform Handbook*. Specifically, 126 of the 134 veterans' appointment records that we reviewed and included a return-to-clinic date documented by the provider received follow-up appointments within 30 days of that return-toclinic date.[38] In addition, our review of 20 veterans discharged from inpatient mental health units at the four VAMCs we visited that provided inpatient mental health care found that these veterans received an outpatient follow-up within 2 days of discharge, on average, and all but one received this follow-up within 7 days of discharge.[39] However, our review found that not all veterans received evidence-based PTSD therapy. Out of the 51 veterans with a diagnosis of PTSD whose records we reviewed, 7 entered into PTSD evidence-based treatment and 44 did not. Mental health providers we interviewed said veterans with PTSD do not always receive these treatments because providers a) do not feel the veteran is appropriate for this intensive treatment, b) have limited availability in their schedule for this level of intensive treatment and, as a result, only select the candidates mostly likely to succeed, or c) the veteran declines.[40]

VHA Monitors Access to Mental Health Care, but Current Policies Cannot Ensure Reliable Data, Which Precludes Effective Oversight

VHA monitors access to mental health care through on-site reviews of clinic operations and sharing data, internally and externally, on mental health access, but the lack of clear policies for reliable data on veteran wait times and missed opportunities precludes effective oversight.[41] Among other things, VHA's on-site reviews are to

- determine compliance with the policies for mental health care, as defined in the *Uniform Handbook*;
- reduce variability in access and quality of mental health care nationwide; and
- identify best practices and areas for growth at each VAMC.

We reviewed the findings of the most recent VHA on-site review for each of the five VAMCs we visited. VHA's recommendations included having one VAMC clarify local policies for referring veterans to mental health and establishing clear criteria on when veterans who have completed treatment should be discharged to primary care or other providers for ongoing monitoring and maintenance. VHA also recommended that another VAMC revise local policies for addressing veteran "no shows"— when a veteran did not attend their appointment and did not cancel in advance—to be consistent with VHA requirements. Following the visits, VHA requires VAMCs to submit corrective action plans that detail how the recommendations will be implemented. For example, one VAMC's action plan stated that it revised the local no-show policy and trained relevant staff.

VHA officials said they also share data on mental health access, such as appointment wait times and VAMCs' missed opportunities rate, with VISN and VAMC staff through internal VHA websites and with the public through its SAIL and patient access reports. However, our previous work, as well as that of the VA OIG, has shown that VHA wait-time data is unreliable and prone to errors and interpretation.[42] Among other things, we found in

December 2012 that VAMCs were not implementing VHA's scheduling policies in a consistent manner, which led to unreliable wait-time data.[43] While VHA has taken steps to increase training in proper scheduling practices, we found three additional reasons contributing to the unreliability of VHA's mental health care wait-time data, which is inconsistent with federal internal control standards that state management should use and communicate, both internally and externally, quality information to achieve its objectives.[44] These include: (1) the wait-time data-entry process has the potential for errors, (2) data may not be comparable over time, and (3) data may not be comparable across VAMCs. In addition, we found that one VAMC was using a document outside of VHA's scheduling system to track veterans referred for a certain type of mental health clinic.

The wait-time data entry process has the potential for errors. Wait-time data relies on information entered at the time an appointment is scheduled, a process which we found has the potential for errors, including scheduler errors (e.g., entering an incorrect preferred date) that are compounded by high turnover in these positions, limitations with the scheduling system (e.g., the ability to view only appointments that follow a veteran's entered preferred date, not those that fall on the day(s) leading up to that date), and variation in how the preferred date is determined (e.g., providers basing their preferred return-to-clinic date on appointment availability instead of on the veteran's preferred date). For example, we found one case where VHA's system-generated wait-time data was calculated incorrectly, based on our review of the records. We identified that the scheduler did not properly search for the next available appointment and, as a result, the VistA scheduling system incorrectly used the date the appointment was created (as opposed to the veteran's preferred date) to calculate the VHA wait time. VAMC officials said this is an easy mistake to make because of the limitations of VHA's scheduling system.

Officials from all of the VAMCs we visited told us that there is the potential for scheduling errors. As result, they may not always be able to rely on VHA's aggregated wait-time data. Instead, some officials said they need to view individual-level information to monitor timely access, which can be time consuming and burdensome. Specifically, officials from one VAMC said that each day they review all scheduled appointments to identify and correct scheduling errors that may affect the accuracy of their data. We found in December 2012, that VHA's scheduling policy was unclear and subject to interpretation and this led to difficulty achieving consistent and correct application of the policy by schedulers. As a result, we recommended that

VHA update its scheduling policy or identify wait-time measures that are not subject to interpretation or prone to scheduling error.[45] Until VHA clarifies its scheduling policy so that it is not as subject to interpretation or error, or develops new wait time measures, as we recommended, it is likely to continue to have data errors and may be missing an opportunity to improve the reliability, and thus usefulness, of its data.

Data may not be comparable over time. VHA has changed the definitions used to calculate various mental health wait-time measures; thus, these measures may not be comparable over time. For example, VHA officials said that in fiscal year 2014 the definition of a 'new mental health patient' changed from an individual who had not been seen within a specific mental health clinic, such as the general mental health clinic or PTSD clinic, to an individual who had not been seen in any mental health clinic. According to VHA officials, this change was made because some veterans were being incorrectly flagged as new in the scheduling system if their appointments with their regular providers were scheduled in a different clinic (e.g., general mental health versus PTSD) than normal. A number of VHA officials, including VAMC and VISN officials, told us they were not sure which definitions were in effect at the time of our interviews or gave conflicting answers about which definitions were currently being used, which is contrary to federal internal controls standards that call for management to communicate relevant and reliable information in a timely manner. VHA has not clearly communicated the definitions used or changes to the definitions, which limits the reliability and usefulness of the wait-time data and VHA's ability to use these measures to determine progress in meeting stated objectives for veterans' wait times. Until VHA clarifies how different access measures are defined and calculated, and communicates any changes over time, local and VISN officials are likely to face difficulties accurately assessing wait times, and identifying needed improvements.

Data may not be comparable between VAMCs. In particular, data may not be comparable when VAMCs use open-access appointments (i.e. blocks of time where veterans may see providers without a scheduled appointment). Specifically, two VAMCs we visited often referred veterans to open-access appointments.[46] In these cases, because appointments were not scheduled until veterans came to the VAMC to be seen, the preferred and appointment dates were the same and wait times were calculated as 0 days, regardless of when veterans requested or were referred for mental health care.[47] Additionally in these cases, because appointments were not scheduled prior to veterans showing up for care, the VAMC's missed-opportunity rate may have been lower and may not be comparable to that of other VAMCs that did not use open-access appointments.

We found that one of the VAMCs we visited had a list of veterans referred to open-access appointments rather than being given specific appointments. This list was maintained outside of VHA's scheduling system in a spreadsheet that was not systematically updated. Officials stated the spreadsheet was not used for clinical decision-making. However, the manual maintenance of the list raises concerns about the potential to lose track of veterans who may have needed mental health services more urgently. This VAMC's own documentation stated that there is no system in place to alert providers if a patient did not arrive for an open-access appointment, limiting officials' ability to follow up at least three times in accordance with VHA's policy to contact veterans at least three times if they miss an appointment without canceling, referred to as their no-show policy.[48] To mitigate the risk of lack of follow up for these veterans, VAMC officials told us that prior to being placed on this open-access appointment list, veterans receive a telephone screening by a mental health nurse who determines their risk level, but also to give veterans themselves an opportunity to determine if and when they should be seen.

Of the 644 veterans who were placed on the referral list for open-access appointments at this VAMC in fiscal year 2014 and through February 2015, close to half (278) were reported as not having shown, and were generally either mailed a letter reminding them about the open-access clinic or had no action recorded.[49] We randomly selected 15 of these veterans' medical records for review, and found inconsistencies with the VAMC's application of VHA's no-show policy for veterans that did not attend an appointment. Just over half, 8 veterans, did not receive mental health care through the open access clinic or through an individual appointment. Of these 8 veterans, only 1 was contacted three or more times to remind them of the need to be seen—in accordance with VHA's no-show policy. The other 7 veterans were not adequately contacted and received phone calls, one letter, or no reminders. One of the veterans that did not receive any type of reminder was brought to the emergency department 1 month later by local police stating that he felt suicidal. The veteran was then admitted for inpatient mental health care. Another veteran was referred to an open-access appointment in January 2015, but did not attend an open access appointment and was not in contact with VHA again until the veteran called in May 2015.

VHA does not have guidance that clarifies how open-access appointments should be used, how such appointments should be scheduled, or how veterans referred for these types of appointments should be tracked. This is inconsistent with federal internal controls that call for management to clearly document policies for significant activities to help ensure management's directives are carried out properly. As a result, officials at the VAMCs who used open-access appointments said they were unclear about how they could be used, how they should be entered into VHA's scheduling system, and whether local tracking mechanisms were compliant with VHA scheduling policies. Officials from one of these VAMCs also said that while they referred some veterans to open-access appointments, they also began giving these veterans scheduled appointments after VHA officials told them that not providing scheduled appointments may not comply with VHA's scheduling policy.[50] In addition, VHA officials said they were not aware of uniform guidance about open-access appointments, and that this lack of guidance could explain why different VAMCs use different approaches. Without guidance on how appointment scheduling for open-access clinics is to be managed, VAMCs can continue to implement these appointments inconsistently, and place veterans on lists outside of VHA's scheduling system, potentially leading to serious negative health outcomes for veterans that need mental health care.

VHA's Hiring Initiative Met Goals, but VAMCs Reported Continued Challenges in Hiring Mental Health Staff and Meeting the Growing Demand for Mental Health Care

VHA's Hiring Initiative Met Its Goals, but VAMCs Reported Continued Challenges Hiring and Placing Mental Health Providers

VHA increased mental health staff at its facilities nationwide through a two-part hiring initiative: (1) VHA's recruitment effort focused on hiring 1,600 new mental health professionals, 300 new non-clinical support staff (such as scheduling clerks), and filling existing vacancies starting in June 2012; and (2) Executive Order 13265, issued in August 2012, which authorized the hiring of 800 peer specialist positions by December 31, 2013, along with reiterating VHA's goal of hiring 1,600 new mental health professionals by June 30, 2013. As a result of this initiative, which included both inpatient and outpatient mental health positions, VHA hired about 5,300 new clinical and non-clinical mental health staff.[51] In particular, VHA hired:

- 1,667 new mental health staff (as of June 30, 2013);
- 304 non-clinical support staff (as of June 30, 2013);
- 2,357 staff to fill existing mental health vacancies and any vacancies that opened during the initiative (as of June 30, 2013); and
- 932 peer specialists (as of December 31, 2013). [52]

VHA hired various types of mental health staff to fill positions under the agency's hiring initiative. (See table 4.) Many hires were for social workers and psychologists, positions that officials at VAMCs we visited reported hiring as part of the hiring initiative.

Table 4. Number of Mental Health Staff Hired under Veterans Health Administration's (VHA) Hiring Initiative, by Occupation Type, as of June 2013

Occupation	New position hires	Vacancy hires	Total hires
Social workers	412	584	996
Mental health nurse	372	616	988
Psychologists	437	321	758
Psychiatrists	155	250	405
Other: clinical[a]	291	413	704
Other: non-clinical[b]	304	173	477
Peer specialists[c]	932	N/A	932
Total	2903	2357	5260

Source: VHA. | GAO-16-24

Notes: Total staff hired does not reflect the total number of staff on board in their positions as of June 30, 2013, as some staff may have left their positions prior to the end of the hiring initiative, necessitating additional hiring.

N/A=Not available

[a]Other: clinical positions include licensed marriage and family therapists, licensed professional mental health counselors, and other mental health professionals.

[b]Other: non-clinical positions include occupations that provide services which facilitate care to the veteran, such as medical support assistants and scheduling clerks.

[c]The total number of peer specialist hires includes staff hired as part of the hiring initiative as well as staff that were hired as part of VHA's regular hiring process. Peer specialist data are as of December 31, 2013.

Officials at the five VAMCs we visited reported local improvements in access to mental health services due to the additional hiring. For example, officials at one VAMC reported being able to offer more evidence-based therapies as a result of the additional hiring. Officials at this VAMC, as well as officials at a second VAMC and two CBOCs, reported being able to provide mental health care at new locations where they were unable to do so prior to the hiring initiative. For example, prior to the hiring initiative, officials at one VAMC said one of their CBOCs had no capacity to provide mental health therapy services. As a result of the hiring, VAMC officials were able to add a psychologist at that CBOC who now provides mental health therapy and testing services for veterans who visit that location.

Further, officials at four of the five VAMCs we visited cited the benefits of having the additional peer specialist hires to assist mental health professionals in performing a variety of therapeutic and supportive tasks with fellow veterans. Peer specialists at the facilities we visited said they educate veterans on available mental health services, provide peer counseling, engage veterans who are resistant to discussing mental health issues, model effective coping techniques, and co-facilitate therapy groups. While VAMC officials cited the benefits of the peer specialists, they also said they initially did not receive clear guidance from VHA on their intended role and thus were unsure how to incorporate the position into the provision of mental health care. Consequently, officials said it took more time to take full advantage of these newly hired positions.

Although VHA considered their hiring initiative a success, officials at the five VAMCs we visited reported a number of challenges in hiring and placing mental health providers, including

- **Pay disparity with the private sector.** Officials at all the VAMCs we visited said that VHA salaries for mental health professionals were not competitive with private sector salaries. For example, officials at one VAMC said they experienced difficulties in recruiting mental health staff, such as psychiatrists, and lost prospective hires to the private sector.
- **Competition among VAMCs.** Officials at three of the five VAMCs we visited also stated that, because every VAMC across the country was trying to fill mental health staff positions at the same time during the hiring initiative, competition among the different VAMCs was high. For example, officials at one VAMC said they made offers to candidates who then used those offers as leverage to secure higher offers at other VAMCs.

- **Lengthy hiring process.** Even when candidates were available to fill positions, officials at four of the five VAMCs we visited stated that VHA's lengthy hiring process—which could take anywhere from 3 months to more than 1 year—was a challenge, possibly resulting in losing candidates who took positions elsewhere during that time. Officials at one VAMC attributed the delays to a lack of human resources staff to complete the administrative side of the hiring process. Despite the VAMC's staff growing significantly as a result of VHA's hiring initiatives, officials said the VAMC did not hire any additional human resources staff, which increased the workload of existing staff and contributed to hiring delays.
- **Lack of space.** Once the hiring process was completed, officials at four of the five VAMCs and all five CBOCs we visited reported difficulties getting mental health hires in place to provide care due to a lack of sufficient space. All of the VAMCs we visited had either recently completed or were in the process of undergoing expansions of mental health space in their VAMC or CBOC buildings. Officials at one of the CBOCs we visited said that although they moved into their current facility in July 2014, by April 2015, they were already struggling with space constraints.
- **Lack of support staff.** Four VAMCs we visited reported that a lack of non-clinical support staff resulted in providers taking on some of the administrative burden, which reduced their clinical availability. For example, officials at one VAMC said that while the recent hiring initiatives added staff to improve access, without a corresponding initiative for hiring support staff, providers are now also scheduling patient appointments, addressing office equipment issues, and handling phone calls about administrative issues, in addition to their clinical duties.
- **Nationwide shortage of mental health professionals.** Officials at three VAMCs we visited reported that the nationwide shortage in mental health professionals also presented a hiring challenge. According to the Department of Health & Human Services' (HHS) Substance Abuse and Mental Health Services Administration, the nation faces a current shortage in the mental health and addiction services workforce, and that shortage is expected to continue.[53] As of July 2015, there were about 4,000 areas designated as having a shortage of mental health professionals, which HHS's Health Resources and Services Administration projected would require

almost 2,700 additional mental health providers to fill the need in these underserved areas.[54]

Additional staff likely will be needed to meet VHA's continuing demand for mental health care. In an April 2015 report, VHA projected a roughly 12 percent increase in mental health staff would be needed to maintain the current veteran staffing ratios for fiscal years 2014-2017.[55] As of March 2015, VHA's mental health staff vacancy rate (14 percent) was similar to that of VHA's overall staff vacancy rate (16 percent), even though the vacancy rates were calculated differently.[56] Mental health staff vacancy rates varied widely among VAMCs we visited, from 9 to 28 percent.[57] Four of the five VAMCs we visited had mental health staff vacancy rates that were higher than the national average. (See table 5.)

Table 5. Mental Health Staff Vacancy Rates Nationally and at Selected VA Medical Centers (VAMC), as of March 2015

VAMC	Number of vacancies	Vacancy rate (percentage)
National	4,147	14
A	63	28
B	53	16
C	13	28
D	13	22
E	23	9

Source: Veterans Health Administration. | GAO-16-24

Note: Vacancies are measured in full-time equivalents. A full-time equivalent is a measure of staff hours equal to those of an employee who works 2,080 hours per year, or 40 hours per week for 52 weeks. Vacancies include both inpatient and outpatient staff positions, and only those administrative positions included in VHA's hiring initiative. The director of the office responsible for maintaining the vacancy data told us that these data may include some staff time used for clinical, research, teaching, and administrative activities.

To address some of the mental health hiring challenges, VAMCs reported using various recruitment and retention tools, including hiring and retention bonuses, student debt repayment, hiring telehealth providers at VHA facilities outside of the region (e.g., a provider located in another state), and using internships and academic affiliations to find potential recruits. For example, officials at one VAMC reported using relocation and recruitment bonuses up to 15 percent of the base salary (usually around $5,000) to recruit mental health clinicians. In November 2014, VHA raised the annual salary ranges for all physicians system-wide, including psychiatrists, to enhance the agency's recruiting, development, and retention abilities when compared with the private sector.[58]

VHA's Hiring Initiative Coincided with an Increased Demand for Mental Health Care That VAMCs Reported Being Unable to Meet

Officials at four of the five VAMCs we visited stated that they were still unable to meet overall demand for mental health care despite VHA's hiring initiative. In addition, an official from a VHA office tracking mental health staffing and access data had not observed any systemic reduction in wait times or staff-to-patient ratios nationally, in part because of simultaneous increased demand for mental health care. Nationally, VHA outpatient mental health staffing totals increased from 11,138 full-time equivalents in fiscal year 2010 to 13,795 in fiscal year 2014, a 24 percent increase.[59] Over the same time period, the number of veterans receiving outpatient mental health care increased from 1,259,300 to 1,533,600, a 22 percent increase. The 22 percent increase in veterans receiving outpatient mental health care has outpaced general growth in the number of veterans using VHA services overall. During the same time period, from fiscal year 2010 through fiscal year 2014, the total number of veterans who used any VHA services increased 9 percent, from 5,441,059 to 5,955,725.[60] VHA attributed the increased demand for mental health care to the influx of veterans returning from the recent conflicts in Iraq and Afghanistan, increased proactive screening efforts, and VHA's increased capacity to provide mental health care

Officials at the five VAMCs we visited described strategies they used to manage demand for mental health care in light of staffing challenges:

- **Changing the type of mental health care offered.** To maintain access given the increased demand, VAMC officials told us they increased the use of telehealth, group therapy (rather than individual therapy), and lengthened the time between therapy appointments. Officials at three of the five VAMCS we visited stated they have increased the use of telehealth to meet the increased demand for mental health services that exceeds their capacity, particularly in rural areas where it is more difficult to hire staff. For example, officials at one VAMC stated that a psychiatrist position has remained open for 2 years at a rural CBOC that has experienced significant increased demand for mental health care. Because of the difficulty in getting that position filled, VAMC officials hired a psychiatrist located in another state to provide mental health care via telehealth to veterans visiting that CBOC. Further, officials at four VAMCs we visited said they refer veterans to group therapy due to shortages in the availability of individual therapy appointments. Finally, officials at three VAMCs and two CBOCs we visited reported shortening appointments or spacing out follow-up individual therapy appointments at longer intervals than what providers preferred. For example, officials at one VAMC we visited said that when they are short staffed, they use shorter appointment times than they would prefer (e.g., 30 minutes) or extend the time between follow-up appointments, which means they did not see patients as often as the providers would prefer.

- **Countering space and staffing constraints.** VAMC officials reported using several strategies to address space shortages such as office sharing, increased teleworking or altering provider schedules, and converting closets into small offices. Officials at one VAMC told us they had designated one provider just for new patient intake appointments. This provider's schedule was made up of 90 minute time slots devoted to assessing the acuity of new patients and referring them to the appropriate source of care. Officials at another VAMC we visited told us they made use of limited office space for individual therapy appointments by having their providers record patient notes in common areas.
- **Referring veterans to other VA locations when a preferred CBOC is not available.** Officials at two VAMCs we visited said that when veterans are unable to receive timely care at their preferred CBOC location, they refer that veteran to the VAMC or another CBOC for care until space becomes available at their preferred location. These two VAMCs had a total of 175 veterans on their transfer lists at the time of our visits. We reviewed 30 of these 175 veterans' records and found 26 veterans were waiting for care at a preferred location and 4 veterans were placed on this list in error. Of the 26 veterans that were waiting for care at a preferred CBOC, 17 were receiving care at other VAMCs or CBOCs until capacity became available at their preferred CBOC and 9 were not. Of the 9 veterans not receiving care at another

location, 7 veterans' records clearly documented that they refused care at an alternative location and 2 veterans' records did not clearly document if they refused alternate care. According to officials at one CBOC, VAMC social workers followed up every month with veterans who opted not to receive care at the VAMC and instead wait for an opening at the preferred CBOC to assess their current mental health status.

VHA's Community Provider Pilot Program Expanded Access to Mental Health Care for a Limited Number of Veterans; VAMCs Reported Successes and Challenges

VHA's Community Provider Pilot Program Provided Mental Health Care for a Limited Number of Veterans

In 2013, 10 VAMCs across VHA established partnerships with 23 community mental health clinics (CMHCs), as required by an August 2012 Executive Order in an effort to help VHA meet veterans' mental health needs; these CMHCs provided mental health care to a limited number of veterans.[61] The over 2,400 mental health appointments that veterans received through the CMHCs accounted for approximately 2 percent of the total mental health care provided across the 10 VAMCs. The most common service veterans received was individual therapy or counseling, but other commonly provided services included group therapy, medication management, and treatment for substance abuse (including intensive outpatient treatment and 28-day residential programs).

Veterans were generally satisfied with the care they received from the CMHCs in the pilot, according to VHA's survey. Veterans who were referred between January 2013 and December 2013 were surveyed retrospectively and 61 percent were completely or somewhat satisfied with the care they received and 19 percent were completely or somewhat dissatisfied.

Most of the 10 VAMCs established partnerships with one or two CMHCs, although one of the participating VAMCs, Atlanta, established seven partnerships.[62] As such, nearly half of the care provided through the pilot program was through partnerships with the Atlanta VAMC.[63] The Atlanta CMHCs provided 1,150 appointments to veterans, while the partnerships with other VAMCs generally provided far fewer appointments. For example, the Indianapolis and Mountain Home VAMCs' partnerships provided the next highest number of appointments, with 664 and 170 appointments respectively, while certain CMHCs that partnered with the Sioux Falls VAMC provided fewer than 10 appointments. (See table 6 for additional information on the community provider pilot sites.)

Table 6. Details of the Community Provider Pilot Program

VA Medical Center	Number of Community Mental Health Clinic pilot partnerships	Number of unique veterans referred for care	Number of veteran appointments
Alaska	1	20	61
Atlanta	7	1418	1150
Biloxi	1	10	20
Central Iowa	1	60	39
Indianapolis	1	Not available[a]	664
Lexington	1	33	168
Mountain Home	2	141	170
Sioux Falls	5	84	63
Tomah	1	13	82
Nebraska-Western Iowa	3	1	12
Total	23	1780	2429

Source: Veterans Health Administration. | GAO-16-24

[a]The Indianapolis VAMC was not able to provide the number of referrals because it did not begin specifically tracking these referrals until recently.

The most common partnership between VAMCs and CMHCs was for the CMHC to provide care on a fee basis. This type of arrangement was used for 12 CMHCs. Payments under fee-basis care are made to non-VA health care providers on an individual veteran basis. The seven CMHCs that partnered with the Atlanta VAMC provided care through locally negotiated contracts, which established the specific services to be provided to veterans. Finally, four CMHCs established partnerships through which VHA mental health providers, located elsewhere, provided telemental health care to veterans at designated CMHCs that were closer to veterans' homes than either the nearest VAMC or CBOC.

While the pilot program has ended, some VAMCs continued their partnerships with affiliated CMHCs.[64] When the pilot ended, the funding for the partnerships ended as well. VAMCs that continued their partnerships had to identify new funding sources, and in general, staff reported that they funded the ongoing partnerships through their normal funding mechanisms. For example, officials from the Atlanta VAMC said that they used money from their discretionary budget to fund the care provided by the CMHCs after the pilot ended. VAMC officials who ended their relationship with CMHCs generally reported that they did so due to a perceived lack of veterans' interest.

Officials Identified Successes and Challenges of the Community Provider Pilot Program

VHA and CMHC officials described a number of successes and challenges related to the pilot program. Improved capacity and communication were among the community provider pilot successes:

Improved capacity. Officials at one VAMC said they would not be able to maintain mental health access at current levels without the capacity provided by the pilot sites. Additionally, officials at three VAMCs said their partnerships allowed them to expand access by providing additional and more convenient care to veterans living in rural areas. Specifically, officials from one of these VAMCs said that, prior to their telemental health partnership with a CMHC, some veterans traveled 2 or more hours to receive care, but using the CMHC drastically reduced veterans' travel times and the VAMC's travel reimbursement costs.[65] Similarly, many veterans reported that they were able to receive care at CMHCs that were much closer than the nearest VAMC or CBOC, according to a VHA survey. VHA's survey also found that approximately 80 percent of veterans reported travel times of more than 30 minutes to the nearest VAMC, while approximately 50 percent reported that traveling to the nearest CMHC took less than 30 minutes.

Improved communication. Both VAMC and CMHC officials said that having a VAMC liaison on site or a dedicated point of contact improved communication. Specifically, one VAMC used previously established relationships with CMHCs to identify pilot sites, and used the pilot program to embed liaisons, who are VAMC employees, which helped facilitate communication between the VAMC and CMHCs. Embedded liaisons, who were registered nurses, were responsible for veteran outreach, the resolution of complaints, and ensuring veterans were receiving care comparable to that provided by the VAMC. Officials at two other VAMCs improved communication by identifying key points of contact. These points of contact worked to improve communications by centralizing information sharing within the VAMCs and CMHCs and addressing veterans' or other concerns, such as billing confusion.

Challenges with the community provider pilot included a number of administrative issues, as well as concerns about the appropriateness of care:

Medical documentation and billing. Officials at two VAMCs noted difficulty receiving timely medical documentation and CMHC officials we spoke with also described difficulty receiving timely payments from VAMCs. VAMC officials reported that delays in receiving medical documentation could limit the ability of VHA to provide quality care if a veteran returned to the VAMC for care prior to the VAMC receiving their medical documentation. CMHC officials reported waiting, at times for months, for payments or resubmitting paperwork multiple times because the VAMC appeared to have misplaced it. VHA recommends including incentives for timely documentation in their contracts with CMHCs as a best practice, but some VAMC officials noted that they had little leverage when trying to create or use such incentives. For example, officials at one facility said they had very little leverage in obtaining documentation because they could not withhold billing while waiting for documentation.

Technical challenges. Both VAMC and CMHC officials in our review also reported experiencing technical challenges, particularly related to the transfer of medical files and the use of telemental health technology. Two VAMCs reported depending on secure fax to exchange information because the VAMCs and the CMHCs used different computer systems. VHA officials said they plan to provide an internal report to VAMCs recommending, among other things, that VAMCs and CMHCs establish standards and plans for sharing information to reduce the impact on care and workload while ensuring confidentiality.

Confusion among available non-VA programs. Some VAMC officials expressed confusion about the different non-VA medical programs, including the CMHC partnerships, available to veterans. Some of the VAMCs in the pilot program extended their partnerships with the CMHCs after the pilot program's end. A VHA document and VHA officials indicated that PC3 and VCP are now the primary programs for obtaining non-VA care of all kinds, including mental health care, although VAMC officials reported it is not always clear which option should be used. Veterans at a facility that continues to fund ongoing partnerships with CMHCs after the pilot program ended would have at least three options for non-VA care (with PC3 and VCP being the primary options). VAMC officials also reported that some providers and patients were unaware of the CMHCs as a treatment option for mental health care and that there is also confusion among patients regarding which services VHA will pay for at non-VA facilities. VHA officials said that veterans generally work with providers to identify the most appropriate non-VA option for mental health care. VHA central office officials said they leave non-VA care decisions up to the individual VAMCs and generally do not review their non-VA care coordination decisions. Previous reports from us and others have highlighted inefficiencies in non-VA care delivery.[66]

Concern about appropriateness of care. VAMC and VISN officials also expressed concern about the appropriateness and effectiveness of referring to community providers for mental health care, and had concerns about the ability of community providers to provide culturally competent and high-quality care to veterans.[67] VAMC and CMHC officials noted the importance of having providers provide culturally competent mental health care for veterans, and some VAMCs were reported to have provided such training to community providers. Some VHA officials expressed concern about whether sufficient providers in certain areas have the necessary training and experience to treat certain types of veterans and one VAMC established guidelines regarding which veterans were eligible to be referred for non-VA care and which were not.[68] VAMC officials said that some veterans preferred receiving care through VHA rather than through a CMHC. Together these factors may have contributed to veterans generally choosing to remain within the VHA system for mental health care. Finally, veterans referred to a CMHC did not always receive care, for a variety of reasons, including that some veterans did not want to receive mental health care once they were referred or veterans did not show up for scheduled appointments.[69]

CONCLUSION

Our review found that veterans at the selected sites were generally receiving mental health care within 30 days of their preferred dates. A veteran's preferred date is the basis for how VHA calculates wait times, although this approach may not accurately reflect veterans' overall wait times. In particular, the way in which VHA calculates the key wait-time measure for new veterans generally does not account for the full amount of time it takes veterans to receive their full mental health evaluations, which we found ranged from 0 days to more than 200 days from their initial requests or referrals. VHA officials told us they are aware that the wait-time calculation does not include some portions of a veteran's wait, but said there is not currently consensus on what standard should be used to begin or end this calculation.

In addition, we found that VHA management of mental health care, as demonstrated through the use of clear policies and accurate measurement of performance, could be improved in three areas. First, the existence of two conflicting access policies (14 days versus 30 days) for a full mental health evaluation, the primary entry point for mental health care, creates confusion among VAMC officials and providers about which policy they are expected to meet. By issuing clarifying guidance, VHA would eliminate confusion and improve VAMC officials' ability to make decisions to prioritize and improve access. Second, VHA lacks guidance on open-access appointments, which has caused confusion about these appointments at the local level and may have contributed to some VAMCs not complying with VHA's scheduling policies. The lack of guidance on open-access appointments also could lead to inconsistent application of VHA's access policies, hinder VHA's ability to assure all veterans are getting their needs served, and may skew the performance measurements of VAMCs that use them—specifically wait-time data and no-show rates—which would result in data that is not comparable across VAMCs. Third, a key way in which VHA measures access to mental health care is through the use of wait-time data. However, our interviews with local and VISN officials confirmed confusion about what definitions are in effect when calculating wait-time measures. The lack of guidance on the calculation of these measures limits their reliability and usefulness. Until VHA clarifies how different access measures are defined and calculated and communicates any changes over time, local and VISN officials are likely to face difficulties accurately assessing wait times and identifying needed improvements.

Finally, our interviews with mental health appointment schedulers and review of medical records confirmed our previous findings about how the wait-time measures are subject to error. As a result, we are reiterating our previous recommendation that VHA take actions to improve the reliability of wait-time measures by clarifying the scheduling policy or identifying clearer wait-time measures that are not subject to interpretation or prone to scheduler error.

RECOMMENDATIONS FOR EXECUTIVE ACTION

To enhance VHA's oversight of veteran mental health care and, in particular, improve and ensure the accuracy, reliability, and usefulness of its mental health data, we recommend that the Secretary of Veterans Affairs direct the Under Secretary for Health to take the following three actions:

- Issue clarifying guidance on which of its access policies (e.g., 14 day or 30 day) should be used for scheduling new veterans' full mental health evaluations.
- Issue guidance on how appointment scheduling for open-access appointments are required to be managed.
- Issue guidance about the definitions used to calculate wait times, such as how a new patient is defined, and communicate any changes in wait-time data definitions within and outside VHA.

AGENCY COMMENTS AND OUR EVALUATION

VHA provided written comments on a draft of this report. In its comments, VHA concurred with our three recommendations and described the agency's plans to implement each, but disagreed with certain findings.

In its comments, VHA stated that with regard to our first recommendation, the agency is in the process of revising the relevant access policy in the *Uniform Handbook* for scheduling full mental health evaluations to be consistent with the 30-day wait time goal the agency established in response to the Choice Act. VHA stated that it has already changed its data metrics and processes for measuring wait time to align with the 30- day goal, is in the process of revising the policy, and has plans to issue clarifying guidance about the policy revisions, metrics, and expectations for scheduling mental health evaluations. VHA plans to publicize this information through national calls and set a target completion date of March 2016.

With regard to our second recommendation, VHA stated that it conducted training in summer 2015 for schedulers based on existing VHA policy that included instructions on how to schedule same-day appointments, which VHA considers to include open-access appointments. However, VHA's description of same-day appointments for individuals who need an initial mental health evaluation, which is to occur within 24 hours of a request or referral for mental health services, does not accurately represent what we observed at two VAMCs during our review. At one of these VAMCs, veterans that expressed a desire or were referred for mental health services received their initial mental health evaluation over the phone, and then, rather than being given a scheduled appointment for the full mental health evaluation, were referred to the open-access clinic to subsequently seek care. We found that close to half of the veterans at this VAMC who were referred to the open-access clinic never showed up at the clinic and follow-up was often inadequate. At the second VAMC, we found that veterans were referred to the open-access clinic, but also were given scheduled appointments for a future date. We have reviewed the training provided to schedulers, as provided by VHA, and it was unclear whether the type of same-day, walk-in appointments addressed by the training would apply to what we observed in the field. Moreover, given potential differences between certain types of walk-in appointments (e.g., walk-in clinics where no prior evaluation may be required and open-access clinics that include an evaluation prior to referral), issuing specific guidance for open-access appointments would help ensure veterans are getting their needs served and that data are comparable when VAMCs use different approaches.

With regard to our third recommendation, VHA provided an overview of the different places that data pertaining to wait times are released. VHA stated that it plans to provide an updated data definition document in October 2015 for the SAIL data and will issue an information letter in November 2015 that contains sources where the general public and VHA employees can find the definitions used to calculate wait times, including how a new patient is defined.

More generally, VHA stated that the draft report does not capture the many ways in which VHA ensures veterans receive the care they need when they want it. In particular, VHA commented that our approach did not highlight an initial assessment which veterans are to receive within 24 hours of initial contact. Although this assessment is discussed in the report, we did not use this measure because, according to VHA officials with whom we spoke, this information is not tracked consistently in VHA's medical record system. We clarified this point in the final report. We believe the report captures various ways VHA provides mental health care, including care provided in outpatient and inpatient settings.

In addition, VHA commented that the use of the preferred date provides meaningful data on wait times because it differentiates between the ideal date a veteran wants to be seen and those dates that are either before or after the veteran's preferred date. VHA commented further that they disagreed with our calculations of the overall time it takes for veterans to receive full mental health evaluations, because it would not capture situations outside of their control such as when a veteran wants to delay treatment. The preferred date is intended to take into account veterans' preferences. However, our calculations illustrate that the use of the preferred date does not always reflect how long veterans are waiting for care or the variation that exists not only between, but within, VAMCs. The report recognizes that many factors could impact a veteran's wait time, including the veteran's preference. Further, we do not recommend a specific method for calculating wait times. Rather, our calculations included the time that a veteran waited after initially requesting or being referred for care, but before an appointment is scheduled, at which time the preferred date is set. During the period of time prior to establishing the preferred date, we found instances of veterans' requests or referrals for care being mismanaged or lost in the system, leading to delays in veterans' access to mental health care. Given the potential vulnerability of veterans seeking mental health care, we believe this time is an important part of the veteran's overall experience that provides meaningful information for VHA. Our current and previous work, along with the work of VA OIG, highlights the limitations of VHA's current scheduling practices, leading us to reiterate our previous recommendation that VHA take actions to improve the reliability of wait-time measures by clarifying the scheduling policy or identifying clearer wait-time measures that are not subject to interpretation or prone to scheduler error.

VHA also commented that the full mental health evaluation should be considered the start of a veteran's treatment, and that therefore there is no delay in care between this evaluation and the delivery of specific interventions. However, during the course of our work, we found a lack of consensus among VHA officials on the appropriate standard or measure for calculating the beginning of treatment. Further, given the wide variation we found across VAMCs in the average number of days between a veteran receiving a full evaluation and their first treatment, as discussed in the report, we believe this presents an important opportunity for VHA to improve veterans' experiences in accessing mental health care.

Finally, VHA commented that our review did not extend to a clinical medical record review to assess quality of care. A full clinical medical record review was beyond the scope of our work. Our objectives in reviewing a selection of veterans' files were to examine veterans' access to and VHA's oversight of timely mental health care. Our review allowed us to address both objectives and provide recommendations for improving veterans' access to mental health care.

Debra A. Draper
Director, Health Care

End Notes

[1] Department of Veterans Affairs, Volume II Medical Programs and Information Technology Programs Congressional Submission Fiscal Year 2016 Funding and Fiscal Year 2017 Advance Appropriations Request (Washington, D.C.).

[2] See Department of Veterans Affairs, Volume II Congressional Submission Fiscal Year 2016 Funding. The 2014 federal fiscal year ended on September 30, 2014. As a result, recent programs that provide additional options for non-VA care to veterans are not included in this amount.

[3] See GAO, VA Health Care: Management and Oversight of Consult Process Need Improvement to Help Ensure Veterans Receive Timely Outpatient Specialty Care, GAO-14-808 (Washington, D.C.: Sept. 30, 2014); VA Health Care: Reliability of Reported Outpatient Medical Appointment Wait Times and Scheduling Oversight Need Improvement, GAO-13-130 (Washington, D.C.: Dec. 21, 2012); VA Mental Health: Number of Veterans Receiving Care, Barriers Faced, and Efforts to Increase Access, GAO-12-12 (Washington, D.C.: Oct. 14, 2011); and VA Faces Challenges in Providing Substance Use Disorder Services and Is Taking Steps to Improve These Services for Veterans, GAO-10-294R (Washington, D.C.: Mar. 10, 2010) . See also Department of Veterans Affairs, Office of Inspector General, Veterans Health Administration: Review of Veterans' Access to Mental Health Care, Report No. 12-00900-168 (Washington, D.C.: Apr. 23, 2012).

[4] See GAO-13-130. We made recommendations to improve oversight of the process for scheduling veterans for outpatient health care, which, along with VHA's actions to address them, are discussed later in this report.

[5] Executive Order No. 13625, 3 C.F.R. 302 (Aug. 31, 2012): Improving Access to Mental Health Services for Veterans, Service Members, and Military Families.

[6] Pub. L. No. 113-146, 128 Stat. 1754 (Aug. 7, 2014).

[7] Outpatient specialty mental health care generally refers to mental health services provided by a mental health specialist (e.g. psychiatrist, psychologist, social worker, or counselor) in an outpatient setting (i.e., receiving medical treatment without being admitted to a hospital) for mental illnesses including schizophrenia, bipolar disorder, PTSD, and substance abuse.

[8] We will refer to the selected VAMCs as VAMCs A through E.

[9] VHA categorizes VAMCs according to complexity level, which is determined on the basis of the characteristics of the patient population, clinical services offered, educational and research missions, and administrative complexity.

[10] In addition to VAMCs, VHA operates CBOCs that are located in areas surrounding VAMCs and provide primary care, and some specialty care services that do not require a hospital stay.

[11] Each of VA's 21 VISNs is responsible for managing and overseeing medical facilities within a defined geographic area.

[12] Vet Centers are community-based centers, owned and operated by the VA, that provide a broad range of counseling, outreach, and referral services to eligible veterans. Veteran service organizations are private, non-profit groups that advocate on behalf of veterans.

[13] Specifically, we sampled veterans who were new to mental health care (new veterans) between July 1 and September 30, 2014. New veterans are individuals who have not received mental health care through VHA within the past 24 months.

[14] We reviewed the timeliness in which veterans received follow-up mental health appointments in the three main mental health clinics: psychiatry, psychology, and substance abuse. Some veterans may receive ongoing care from multiple providers.

[15] We randomly sampled veterans who were discharged from inpatient mental health stays between July 1 and September 31, 2014.

[16] Based on the most recent data available, as of May 2015, a total 644 veterans were placed on this list in fiscal year 2014 and through February 2015.

[17] See GAO, Standards for Internal Control in the Federal Government, GAO/AIMD-00-23.3.1 (Washington, D.C.: Nov. 1999). Internal control is synonymous with management control and comprises the plans, methods, and procedures used to meet missions, goals, and objectives.

[18] Transfer lists are lists that select VAMCs use to manage the transfer of veterans from one VHA facility to another.

[19] According to the Substance Abuse and Mental Health Services Administration, mental health recovery is a process of change through which individuals improve their health and wellness, live a self-directed life, and strive to reach their full potential. See Department of Health and Human Services, Substance Abuse and Mental Health Services Administration, Working Definition of Recovery (Rockville, MD: Feb. 2012).

[20] Department of Veterans Affairs, Uniform Mental Health Services in VA Medical Centers and Clinics, Veterans Health Administration Handbook 1160.01, (Washington, D.C.: Sept. 11, 2008).

[21] Cognitive processing therapy helps patients gain an understanding of, and modify the meaning attributed to their traumatic events. Prolonged exposure therapy is characterized by re-experiencing a traumatic event in order to become less sensitive to the traumatic memories, and reducing the stress and avoidance behaviors associated with remembering the traumatic events.

[22] VHA outpatient medical appointment scheduling policy is documented in Department of Veterans Affairs, VHA Outpatient Scheduling Processes and Procedures, VHA Directive 2010-027, (Washington, D.C.: June 9, 2010). For the purposes of this report, we refer to the directive as "VHA's scheduling policy".

[23] VistA is the single integrated health information system used throughout VHA in all of its health care settings. VHA officials said they revised the previously used term "desired date" to "preferred date," although these terms refer to the same field within VistA.

[24] The Choice Act defines wait-time goals for VHA as not more than 30 days from the date on which the veteran requests an appointment for services unless VA submits a report and public notice of an alternative policy. On October 17, 2014, VHA specified in the Federal Register a wait-time policy of "not more than 30 days from either the date that an appointment is deemed clinically appropriate, or, if no such determination has been made, the date a veteran prefers to be seen for hospital care or medical services." Previously, VHA referred to this as desired date but now refers to it as preferred date. See 79 Fed. Reg. 62519 (Oct. 17, 2014).

[25] Peer specialists are veterans with mental health conditions who are in recovery and have been trained to help others with mental health conditions.

[26] VA is authorized to obtain health care services from non-VA providers through both the Non-VA Medical Care Program and clinical contracts. VA obtains the services of non-VA providers in non-VA facilities under the following statutory authorities: 38 U.S.C. §§ 1703, 1725, 1728, 8111, and 8153.

[27] PC3 is a nationwide VA program that established two nationwide contracts with Health Net and TriWest to establish networks of providers that can provide care through the Non-VA Medical Care Program in a number of specialties—including primary care, inpatient specialty care, and mental health care.

[28] Pub. L. No. 113-146, § 101 (a), (b), 128 Stat. 1754, 1755-1756 (Aug. 7, 2014).

[29] See the Surface Transportation and Veterans Health Care Choice Improvement Act. Pub. L. No. 114-41, § 4002, 129 Stat. 443, 461 (Jul. 31, 2015).

[30] The Uniform Handbook has an expiration date of September 30, 2013, however, VHA officials told us that it is still in effect and no update has been published.

[31] VHA also has a policy that states that veterans who are new to mental health should receive initial assessments within 24 hours to identify those with urgent care needs. VHA officials told us these assessments can be completed by a number of providers, including the referring provider, and that VHA does not have a way to consistently track them. As a result, VHA does not have a measure to assess whether these initial assessments are being completed in a timely manner.

[32] GAO/AIMD-00-21.3.1.

[33] Most of the veterans whose records we reviewed, 59 of 100, accessed mental health through a primary care referral.

[34] A veteran is to be contacted after an initial request or referral in order to set up an appointment. Part of the appointment scheduling process includes the veteran providing a preferred date for their appointment.

[35] The veteran's request to receive mental health care was not reflected in the preferred date for the appointment 7 months later. The preferred date for that appointment was documented as being the same day as the appointment, reflecting a wait time of 0 days.

[36] See Department of Veterans Affairs, Office of Inspector General, Review of Veterans' Access to Mental Health Care. The OIG recommended that VHA revise the full mental health evaluation measurement to better reflect the veteran's experience from the point of first contact with mental health care to the completion of the full mental health evaluation.

[37] VHA has additional policies that are outside the scope of this engagement, including evidence-based therapies for substance abuse.

[38] Each veteran may have multiple appointment records that included a return-to-clinic date. For the 100 veterans in our sample, we reviewed 77 psychiatry appointments, 52 psychology appointments, and 5 substance abuse appointments with return-to-clinic dates documented

by the provider. Nearly all of these follow-up appointments were completed within 30 days of the return-to-clinic date and we found no significant variation between the specialties.

[39] VHA performance data for the fourth quarter of fiscal year 2014 show that, nationwide, veterans received this follow-up within 7 days of discharge 83 percent of the time. VAMCs nationwide and the four sites we visited exceeded VHA's performance goal of 75 percent in the fourth quarter of fiscal year 2014.

[40] Other research has shown relatively low receipt of evidence-based therapy among veterans with PTSD within VHA, due to a number of factors, including that such therapy is not available at some VAMCs and CBOCs, and not every veteran wants, needs, or meets the treatment criteria for such therapy. See RAND Health, Veterans Health Administration Mental Health Program Evaluation: Capstone Report (Santa Monica, Calif.: Rand Corporation, 2011) and Institute of Medicine of the National Academies, Treatment for Posttraumatic Stress Disorder in Military and Veteran Populations: Final Assessment (Washington, D.C.: National Academies Press, 2014).

[41] In June 2014, VHA completed an access audit of all VAMCs and selected CBOCs, assessing scheduling staff's understanding of VA's policy, identifying any inappropriate scheduling practices used, and reviewing waiting list management. In addition, VHA's Office of Mental Health Operations conducts on-site reviews of VAMCs. Officials told us they visited all VAMCs in 2012, and after that time have visited about a third of all VAMCs each year.

[42] See GAO-13-130, GAO-14-808, and Department of Veterans Affairs, Office of Inspector General, Review of Veterans' Access to Mental Health Care.

[43] In response to these findings, we recommended that VHA take action to ensure VAMCs consistently implement the scheduling policy and ensure that all schedulers take the required training. VHA concurred with the recommendation and reported taking steps, such as drafting a standardized training on scheduling procedures that is to be taken by all schedulers. As of March 2015, VHA was in the process of revising scheduling guidance and training.

[44] See GAO/AIMD-00-21.3.1.

[45] See GAO, VA Health Care: Reliability of Reported Outpatient Medical Appointment Wait Times and Scheduling Oversight Need Improvement, GAO-13-130 (Washington, D.C.: Dec. 21, 2012). VHA concurred with this recommendation and has convened an internal group to revise the scheduling portion of the outpatient scheduling guidance, but as of March 2015, had not published revised guidance.

[46] Officials from these VAMCs told us they refer veterans to open-access appointments who, based on a triage evaluation, are determined to be a low risk for harming themselves or others and who are not in need of an urgent appointment.

[47] According to VHA officials, when aggregate wait times are calculated, appointments with a 0-day wait time are not included in the calculations.

[48] Veterans Health Administration, Guidance on Patient Failure to Attend Appointments (No Shows), VHA Memorandum (Washington, D.C.: Aug. 6, 2013).

[49] The list noted that the remaining 366 veterans were seen in the VAMC's open-access clinic.

[50] Officials said that if patients came to open-access appointments for treatment, their scheduled appointments were generally canceled.

[51] VHA officials told us total staff hired does not reflect the total number of staff on board in their positions as of June 30, 2013, as some staff may have left their positions prior to the end of the hiring initiative, necessitating additional hiring.

[52] The total number of peer specialist hires includes staff hired as part of the hiring initiative, as well as staff that were hired as part of VHA's regular hiring process. VHA could not provide separate numbers for those hired as part of the hiring initiative, and those hired as part of the regular hiring process. The total also includes peer support apprentice hires. Peer support apprentices serve in a developmental capacity until they are certified as peer specialists.

[53] Substance Abuse and Mental Health Services Administration, Report to Congress on the Nation's Substance Abuse and Mental Health Workforce Issues (Washington, D.C.: Jan. 24, 2013).

[54] U.S. Department of Health and Human Services, Health Resources and Services Administration, Bureau of Clinician Recruitment and Service, Designated Health Professional Shortage Area Statistics, as of July 29, 2015 (Washington, D.C.: Jul. 29, 2015).

[55] Department of Defense and Department of Veterans Affairs, DOD/VA Report to the Congress in Response to Senate Report 113-44, pg. 133, Accompanying S. 1197, the National Defense Authorization Act for Fiscal Year 2014: Mental Health Counselors for Service Members, Veterans, and their Families (Washington, D.C.: April 17, 2015).

[56] The mental health staff vacancy rate is calculated based on a survey of VAMC officials, while, according to VHA officials, the overall staff vacancy rate is calculated based on vacancy information entered into VHA's human-resources tracking database.

[57] Vacancies include both inpatient and outpatient staff positions, and only those administrative positions included in VHA's hiring initiative. The director of the VHA office responsible for maintaining the vacancy data told us that these data may include some staff time used for clinical, research, teaching, and administrative activities.

[58] 79 Fed. Reg. 56125 (Sept. 18, 2014). See 38 U.S.C. § 7431, which sets forth requirements for setting salary ranges for VHA physicians and dentists.

[59] A full-time equivalent is a measure of staff hours equal to those of an employee who works 2,080 hours per year, or 40 hours per week for 52 weeks. Full-time equivalent data include time spent on clinical, research, teaching, and administrative activities.

[60] Department of Veterans Affairs, Volume II Medical Programs and Information Technology Programs Congressional Submission Fiscal Year 2012 Funding and Fiscal Year 2013 Advance Appropriations Request (Washington, D.C.); and VA Volume II Congressional Submission Fiscal Year 2016 Funding.

[61] While VHA reported that 12 VAMCs established partnerships with CMHCs, the pilot program at one VAMC was never fully implemented and no veterans were referred to care. Similarly, another VAMC identified two potential sites, but never referred any patients for care.

[62] Atlanta initially established partnerships with five CMHCs but expanded to two additional CMHCs during the course of the pilot program.

[63] Over 90 percent of the 808 veterans surveyed by VHA for the pilot evaluation received services through one of the CMHCs that partnered with the Atlanta VAMC.

[64] Many pilot partnerships began in February or March 2013, though some partnerships were not established until late 2013.

[65] Veterans are eligible to receive reimbursement for some travel expenses associated with medical appointments, such as mileage, if they meet certain criteria, generally related to whether they have a service-connected disability or low income level.

[66] See GAO, VA Health Care: Actions Needed to Improve Administration and Oversight of Veterans' Millennium Act Emergency Care Benefit, GAO-14-175 (Washington, D.C.: Mar. 6, 2014) and VA Health Care: Management and Oversight of Fee Basis Care Need

Improvement, GAO-13-441 (Washington, D.C.: May 31, 2013). We made several recommendations to improve (1) data on wait times and cost-effectiveness of non-VA medical care; and (2) VA's oversight and monitoring of claims processing. VA agreed with these recommendations, and has taken action on some, but has yet to fully implement others. See also, Department of Veterans Affairs Office of Inspector General, Audit of Veterans Health Administration's Non-VA Outpatient Fee Care Program, 08-02901-185 (Washington, D.C.: Aug. 3, 2009). See also National Academy of Public Administration, Veterans Health Administration Fee Care Program (Washington, D.C.: Sept. 2011).

[67] Culturally competent care, for our purposes, refers to the delivery of services by providers that are respectful of and responsive to the experiences, views, and needs of veterans.

[68] While officials acknowledged they made exceptions for certain patients, they generally did not refer patients for non-VA care if they were at a high risk for suicide, had combat veteran status, or had been recently hospitalized for mental health care, among other factors.

[69] Officials at one VAMC noted that they tracked no shows to CMHCs and conducted outreach via telephone and letter to ascertain the veteran's interest and need for mental health care.

In: Veterans' Access to Mental Health Care
Editor: Edgar W. Schneider
ISBN: 978-1-63485-195-4

Chapter 2

STATEMENT OF DR. HAROLD KUDLER, CHIEF CONSULTANT FOR MENTAL HEALTH SERVICES, DEPARTMENT OF VETERANS AFFAIRS. HEARING ON "VA MENTAL HEALTH: ENSURING ACCESS TO CARE"*

Good morning, Chairman Isakson, Ranking Member Blumenthal, and members of the Committee. Thank you for the opportunity to discuss the important topic of access to and timeliness of Veterans' mental health care. I am accompanied by Dr. David Carroll, Executive Director, Mental Health Operations and Dr. Michael Davies, Executive Director, Access and Clinical Administration Program.

VHA MENTAL HEALTH CARE

The Veterans Health Administration's (VHA) mission is to honor America's Veterans by providing exceptional healthcare that improves their health and well-being. Providing timely access to that care is a critical aspect of our mission. Access enables VHA to provide personalized, proactive, patient-driven health care; achieve measurable improvements in health outcomes; and align resources to deliver sustained value to Veterans. VHA is

---

* This is an edited, reformatted and augmented version of a statement presented October 28, 2015 before the Senate Committee on Veterans' Affairs.

continually monitoring wait times and making adjustments as needed to ensure that Veterans have access to the best care they rightfully deserve.

Between 2005 and 2014, the number of Veterans who received mental health care from VA grew by 71 percent. This rate of increase is more than 3 times that seen in the overall number of VA users. The increase in the number of mental health encounters or treatment visits, from 10.5 million in 2005 to 19.6 million in 2014, has been even more dramatic – an 87-percent increase. This reflects VA's concerted efforts to engage Veterans that are new to our system and stimulate better access to MH services for Veterans within our system. These include outreach and engagement through 300 Vet Centers, 70 Mobile Vet Centers, Primary Care/MH Integration at VA Medical Centers, and large community-based clinics. VA Telemental Health innovations provided more than 335,000 encounters to over 108,000 Veterans in 2014. Telemental Health reaches Veterans where and when they are best served. VA is a leader across the US and internationally in these efforts. VA's MaketheConnection.net, Suicide Prevention campaigns, and the PTSD mobile app (which has been downloaded over 208,000 times) add to the increase in MH access and utilization. These efforts align with VA's interagency activities including the Cross Agency Priority (CAP) Goals and expanding VA MH policy and practice. As a result of these trends, the proportion of Veterans served by VA who receive mental health care increased to more than 1.5 million Veterans. In 2005, 19 percent of VA users received mental health services, and in 2014, the figure was 27 percent.

GAO Report

This month the Government Accountability Office (GAO) released a report regarding the need for clearer guidance on access policies and wait time data relating to VA mental health care. VA is committed to providing timely access to high quality, recovery-oriented mental health care that anticipates and responds to Veterans' needs and supports their reintegration into their communities. VA appreciates the GAO review of timely access to mental health care issues at VA Medical Centers (VAMC) and concurs with GAO's recommendations. We take the findings very seriously and have implemented action plans to address the recommendations.

The GAO report found that the way in which VHA calculates mental health wait times may not always reflect the overall amount of time Veterans wait for care. Specifically, GAO notes that a patient who presents with

Mental Health concerns receives an initial evaluation within 24 hours and may not receive a full evaluation until a later date. However, this initial evaluation is the start of treatment. It includes initial diagnostic evaluation and treatment of the most acute problems as appropriate. It may result in a patient being admitted to the hospital, for example, or medication adjustments. At the same time, these patients are often scheduled for a full and comprehensive evaluation at a later time. Of the 100 Veterans whose records GAO reviewed, 86 received full mental health evaluations within 30 days of their preferred date.

The GAO report noted four findings. First, the Veterans' preferred dates were, on average, 26 days after their initial requests or referrals for mental health care, and ranged from 0 - 279 days. Second, the conflicting access policies for a full mental health evaluation - one which mandates a 14-day deadline versus another which allows for 30 days from the Veteran's preferred date - created confusion among VAMC officials about which policy they are expected to follow. Third, GAO found that data may not be comparable over time as the definitions or updated definitions of new patients have not been communicated with VISN and Medical Center leadership and managers. Fourth, GAO found inconsistencies in the implementation of these appointments; including one VAMC that manually maintained a list of Veterans seeking mental health outside of VHA's scheduling system.

GAO recommended three items for action in response to its findings. First, VA should issue clarifying guidance on which of VHA's policies (14 or 30 days) should be used for scheduling new Veterans' full mental health evaluations. Second, VA should issue guidance on how appointment scheduling for open-access appointments is required to be managed. Third, VA should issue guidance about the definitions used to calculate wait times, such as how a new patient is defined, and communicate this to VISN and Medical Center leadership and managers any changes in wait time data definitions.

INCREASING ACCESS AND HIRING PRACTICES

The GAO report found that VHA met Mental Health hiring initiative goals, but that VAMCs reported continued challenges in ongoing hiring of mental health staff and in meeting the increasing demands for such care.

In 2012, VHA began a two-part hiring initiative under Executive Order 13625 issued in August 2012. The first part focused on recruiting 1,600 new mental health professionals, 300 new non-clinical support staff (such as scheduling clerks), and filling existing vacancies as of June 2012. The second part was the hiring of 800 peer specialist positions by December 31, 2013. As a result of this initiative, VHA hired approximately 5,300 new clinical and non-clinical mental health staff. As of the third quarter of fiscal year (FY) 2013, this included 1,667 new mental health staff, 304 non-clinical support staff, and 2,357 staff to fill existing mental health vacancies and those that opened during the initiative. As of December 31, 2013, VHA had hired 932 peer specialists. GAO found that VAMC officials reported local improvements due to the additional hiring, such as more evidence-based therapies offered, mental health care provided at new locations, and a variety of benefits provided by the new peer specialists such as modeling effective coping, engaging Veterans who are resistant to discussing mental health issues, and providing peer-to-peer counseling. VAMC officials also cited several challenges to hiring mental health care providers such as pay disparity with the private sector, competition among VAMCs, the lengthy hiring process, lack of space and support staff, and an underlying nationwide shortage of mental health professionals.

At a national level, VHA outpatient mental health staff totals increased from 11,138 full-time equivalents in 2010 to 13,975 in FY 2014. Over the same time period, the number of Veterans receiving outpatient mental health care increased from 1,259,300 to 1,533,600. The increase in Veterans receiving mental health care outpaced both the related hiring and the overall growth in the number of Veterans using VHA services.

The recent rapid growth in the number of Veterans seeking mental health treatment in VA has posed challenges in the area of staffing. In Figure 1 below, the solid line shows the growth in numbers of Veterans using mental health services, from 897,600 in 2005 to 1,533,600 in 2014. The number of patients is expressed in terms of hundreds to show staff and patient numbers on the same graph. For example, 10,000 on the vertical axis represents 1,000,000 patients and 10,000 full time equivalents employees (FTEs).

This graph also shows the growth in numbers of mental health clinical staff, measured in terms of the FTE providing outpatient and inpatient treatment. Consistent with a shift to outpatient care, the inpatient mental health FTEs began to level off after 2009. Outpatient mental health FTEs began to lag behind the growth in patient numbers in 2012, but as part of the President's 2012 Executive Order 13625, "*Improving Access to Mental Health Service Members, and Military Families,*" VA hired more than 1,600 new clinical providers by the June 30, 2013, target date.

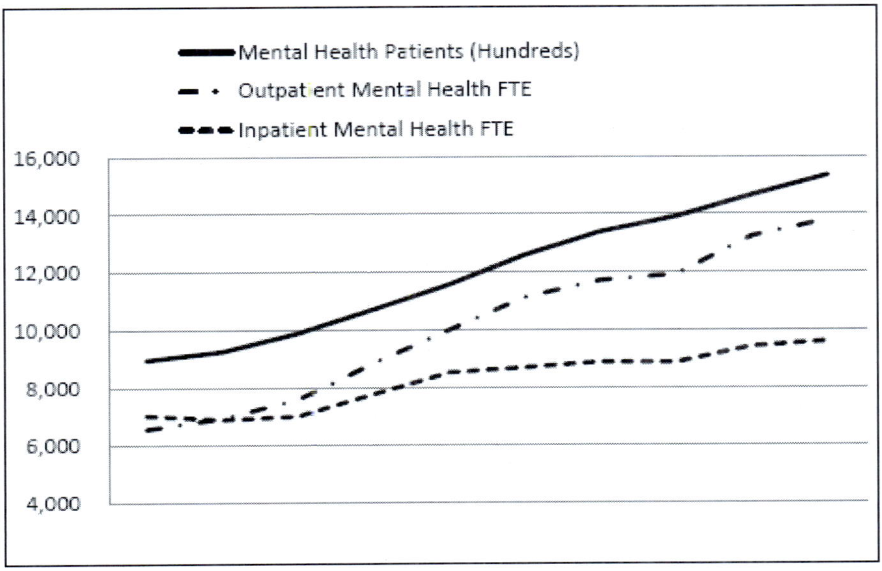

Figure 1. Growth in annual numbers of patients using mental health services and in outpatient and inpatient FTE levels, 2005 to 2014.

In the absence of any national benchmark related to mental health staffing, VA continues to refine a model that is intended to inform local facility decision-making about the number of staff necessary to meet local demand for mental health services. In addition, VA is addressing access through the following efforts:

- Veteran-centered operating hours: Extended hours help increase capacity when space is limited and improve the match between available staff hours and the needs of Veterans who are employed or have other competing responsibilities during day-time hours.
- Leveraging trainees and fellows: These professionals provide substantial amounts of clinical care under the direct supervision of appropriately licensed and privileged mental health staff. Training programs also provide ready access to well-qualified candidates for recruitment into vacant positions.
- Support staff, adjunct professions, and peer support staff: VA has hired over 900 peer specialists and is developing a pilot program in response to the President's August 2014 Executive Actions to expand the role of peer specialists into primary care settings.

COMMUNITY PROVIDER PILOT PROGRAM

In 2013, 12 VA Medical Centers (VAMCs) partnered with 24 Community Mental Health Clinics (CMHCs) across the country to establish Community Mental Health (CMH) pilots. These pilots were created in response to Section 3(a) of Executive Order 13625 which focused on the creation of "Enhanced Partnerships between the Department of Veterans Affairs (VA) and Community Providers" designed specifically to decrease wait times and increase the geographic reach of VA mental health services. Pilot sites were able to select a model of care to best meet the needs of local Veterans. All sites used one of two broad approaches: Non-VA care or VA telemental health (TMH), with most sites choosing to provide Non-VA care to Veterans. Non-VA care uses community providers that are paid by VA. TMH care utilizes technology to deliver mental health services via modalities such as video conferencing and allows for real-time (or "synchronous") encounters between health care providers and patients who are not in the same location. During the VA/CMHC Pilot partnerships, TMH services enabled Veterans to receive care at designated community clinics that were closer to their homes than the nearest VA medical facilities or clinics.

VA and CMHC staff worked together in determining roles and responsibilities within each pilot partnership. Partnerships using telemental health required space, equipment, a technician, and a protocol for handling emergencies (e.g., a Veteran becoming distressed during a TMH session). For Non-VA care partnerships, there were other responsibilities that needed to be addressed: coordination of care (between VA and CMHCs), billing, and payment. While some pilot site VAMCs developed strong systems for coordinating care, monitoring patients, and billing, other sites, especially smaller ones, experienced challenges in these areas.

Evaluation of the pilots included both gathering data from not only Veterans about their experiences, but also from key staff at each of the participating Veterans Integrated Service Networks (VISN) and VA Central Office (VACO) and a review of key documents associated with the pilots. Results from follow up surveys indicate that Veterans were very satisfied with the services they received via these pilots. When the pilots concluded, each participating VAMC was allowed to determine whether to continue the partnership. Since that time, VA has also moved to Patient Centered Community Care, a centralized contracting mechanism, and has implemented the Veteran's Choice Program. Regardless of how such care is provided, the growing Veteran's need for mental health services will increase the need for efficient leveraging of Non-VA community providers when access to care is not available within the VA system of care. VA is rising to the challenge through its Community Mental Health Summit program which engaged over 11,000 individuals at 144 sites in FY 14 and continues annually to bring together DoD, VA, State, and Community providers and stakeholders for vital conversations at the local level. VA and DoD developed a joint Military Cultural Competence Training Program as part of the Integrated Mental Health Strategy which is now housed on the public facing TRAIN website and which, to date, has provided free training to over 2,000 providers. Whether mental health care is delivered directly by Non-VA mental health care providers, through TMH care at Non-VA sites, or any other means, it is critical for VA to continue to provide Veterans with access to high quality mental health care in coordination with other VA services.

VA Response Letter to GAO Report

VA concurred with all of GAO's recommendations in its October 7, 2015, response and added some additional explanation for some of VA's policies.

Regarding the recommendation to clarify guidance on which deadline to use, VA cited VHA Handbook 1160.01, which established that all new patients requesting or referred to mental health services must receive an initial evaluation within 24 hours and a more comprehensive diagnostic and treatment planning evaluation within 14 days. The primary goal of the initial evaluation is to identify patients who require urgent care, such as hospitalization or immediate outpatient care. VHA's policy directs that patients needing mental health care receive clinically indicated care as quickly as possible.

VA explained that the 30-day policy was a result of a goal published in the Federal Register as required by the August 2014 Veterans Access, Choice and Accountability Act. VHA has since revised and tested its metrics and management process and is ready to update its policy to the 30-day standard consistent with the published goal, rather than a 14-day standard developed internal to VA for new mental health patients. Once the policy is updated, VHA will announce it on the appropriate national calls with key stakeholders. The target completion date for this recommendation is March 2016.

For patients who already have a mental health provider who need follow up care, VHA's policy of less than 30 days wait time from a Veteran's preferred dated is consistent with The Veterans Access, Choice and Accountability Act. Therefore, this policy does not require revision.

MANAGEMENT OF OPEN-ACCESS APPOINTMENTS

Open access, also known as same-day scheduling, is a method of scheduling in which all patients can receive an appointment on the day they call in or walk in. VHA's open access is an essential component of VHA's standard of care for conducting an initial mental health evaluation within 24 hours of a Veteran's request for care. As the identification of a Veteran who may need or request mental health services can occur at several entry points to care, each facility must have a defined process that identifies a "warm hand-off" to a professional who can conduct the same-day initial mental health evaluation and arrange any appropriate follow-up.

Open access scheduling for an initial mental health evaluation ensures that if during a visit to a treatment facility, a Veteran requests or is identified as needing a mental health assessment, it will be provided or at least offered to the Veteran who has the option to accept care prior to the Veteran's departure from the facility.

VHA Directive 2010-027, paragraph 4c(1) established the requirements for documenting same day unscheduled appointments. VHA conducted extensive scheduler training this year. To date, more than 23,000 schedulers have undergone training. VHA finds that the combination of current policy and training constitutes clear guidance on how to manage and schedule open access appointments. Many schedulers are still developing proficiency with the training, and therefore there are still occasional errors. VHA continues to aggressively monitor appointment management and identify areas of local inconsistency in scheduling procedures.

VA agrees with GAO's finding that one medical center was using inappropriate processes for scheduling open access appointments. VA continues to work with this facility to ensure their processes are aligned with VHA.

Mr. Chairman, VA is committed to providing the highest quality care our Veterans have earned and deserve. Our work to effectively and timely treat Veterans who desire or need mental health care and ensure Veterans have access to the counseling and care they need continues to be a top priority. We appreciate Congress' support and look forward to responding to any questions you may have.

In: Veterans' Access to Mental Health Care ISBN: 978-1-63485-195-4
Editor: Edgar W. Schneider

Chapter 3

TESTIMONY OF NICHOLAS KARNAZE, VETERAN, U.S. MARINES. HEARING ON "VA MENTAL HEALTH: ENSURING ACCESS TO CARE"*

Mr. Chairman and Members of the Committee,

Thank you for the invitation to be here today; it is an honor to be able to share my experiences with you. My name is Nicholas Karnaze, and I served 7.5 years in the United States Marine Corps both as an intelligence officer and as a special operations officer. I served two combat deployments in Afghanistan, and I have a disability rating with the VA. Because of this, I receive all of my health care through the VA. I am a graduate of the United States Naval Academy, and recently received a certificate from the Stanford University Graduate School of Business.

I am testifying today from the perspective of a veteran with service-connected disabilities who has attempted to receive mental health treatment from the VA. As a leader of Marines, I feel it is my duty to share my personal experiences with you so that, together, we can ensure the men and women who honorably served our nation receive the mental health care that they deserve.

Many men and women are suffering in silence from the mental wounds they sustained during their time in the military. Most know they need help, but some are fearful to ask out of concern that any mention of "mental health" will have an adverse effect on their government security clearance, and ultimately,

* This is an edited, reformatted and augmented version of testimony presented October 28, 2015 before the Senate Committee on Veterans' Affairs.

their jobs. For those who have mustered the courage to reach out, most are confronted with a lengthy and discouraging administrative process in order to gain access to mental health care. There are extremes in mental health – for example if a person is about to commit suicide - but the majority of people seeking treatment have not reached that point.

Often, veterans who are actively seeking help are in the stage in which they experience the feeling that something is not right. While they may know something is wrong, they are not on the verge of suicide, so contacting the VA's widely publicized Veterans Crisis Line seems excessive. So what options do we veterans have in this situation?

Upon leaving active duty, it took me over a year to gain access to the VA healthcare system. Once in the system, the actual physical care I received was fantastic. But, it's the time and process necessary to ultimately receive the care is where the issues lie.

In the fall of 2014 I expressed an interest to meet with a mental health care professional to discuss some issues I'd been having with concentration and memory. Upon referral to a psychiatrist, it took over a month before I was finally able to meet with the doctor. During our hour-long initial meeting, she asked if I was opposed to taking medication, mentioning that while I do not feel depressed, my inability to concentrate could be a symptom of depression. Eager to "get my head right," I said I had no problem trying medication. She then prescribed me an antidepressant, and we agreed to meet several months later to assess my progress. She noted that it could take from several weeks to a month before I noticed a change in my mood.

Two weeks into taking the medication, I began to *feel* depressed, beyond my initial issue with memory and concentration. Cold, lonely depression took its hold. I felt hopeless. At first I thought I was just having a really bad day, but these feelings persisted. I knew something was wrong. This was not me. I attempted to call the VA to talk with the psychiatrist, but she could not see me for about 30 days. I could not live like this for 30 days. I decided to stop taking the medication. Shortly after I stopped taking the drug, my mood began to improve and I was soon back to my original baseline. When I was able to see the doctor again, she said that I had made the right choice in stopping the medication. She asked if I wanted to try a different drug. I declined. I told her I'd like to try cognitive therapy. She said that was a good idea, but could not provide that for me. I was not referred to a psychologist. I left the clinic and that was the last interaction I've had with a VA mental health professional.

My experience in which the VA deferred to pharmaceutical treatment instead of psychological treatment is not unique. On August 26, 2014, Adam

Looney took his own life. Adam was a Marine Corps veteran and brother of my friend Kate Looney, also a Marine Corps veteran. Up until his death, Adam was receiving mental health treatment from the VA in Columbia, MO. According to Kate, the "VA's approach was basically to try every psychiatric medication without really taking the time to counsel the root issue. He used to hate going because it was a long drive and a long wait. I brought him a few times, and he was never in there long. It seemed they were always changing his meds, losing paperwork and switching his counselor."

CURRENT SITUATION

I receive my health care through the VA Community Based Outpatient Clinic at the Ft. Belvoir Community Hospital. Still interested in meeting with a psychologist, I recently attempted to contact my clinic for a referral. The only way I've found to do this is through the one phone number listed on the clinic's website. The phone number links to an audio recording that lists another phone number to call for referrals. After calling that number, I was on hold for about 15 minutes before I decided to select the option of having a representative call me back when one became available. To date, no representative has called me back nor responded to the voice message I left requesting help earlier this week.

From a mental perspective, I feel very fortunate. No matter how bad things get, I always have a slight feeling that everything will be okay, that I just need to keep pushing forward. This feeling has been with me through my most difficult days on the battlefield and during my darkest times at home. Because of it, I have always been able to keep moving. But I know not everyone has this internal voice. When a person reaches out for help, especially mental health help, they are extremely vulnerable. Not having someone pick up on the other end, someone you have been told will help, is crushing. When you are suffering from a mental wound, you will not have the emotional energy to keep asking for help if your first calls go unanswered.

After learning I'd be testifying before you today, I posted on Facebook asking my friends about their experiences with mental health care from the VA. The responses I received were overwhelming. Alisa Beasley emailed me the following:

> I was medically retired from the Army 28 April 2014. I was just barely holding on mentally, that is how I felt. I saw my primary care

provider by May and referred to Mental Health that same day! Then I saw a psychologist in July. Then nothing. I was supposed to be receiving follow up visits and every time I called the Mental Health number it just beeped like it was disconnected. I was so frustrated, and on top of that the VA had sent me a letter stating my benefits would be cut due to two missed appointments for psychiatry and neurology. I didn't miss either of these appointments, they were never rescheduled like I called and asked for. I could literally feel my world crumbling. I had gone through a really tough divorce, he wasn't letting me see my kids...I felt like what's the point. I'm done. I was having panic attacks and nightmares and depression. I called and called and there was never an answer from the VA mental health building. It took me calling the patient advocate. By this time I was a sobbing mess and crying and shaking and felt like my world was crashing. She was kind enough to tell me it looks like they literally just dropped me completely off the mental health log. She was able to get me an appointment for February 2015, this call took place in November 2014. I didn't see a psychiatrist to talk about possibility of meds till sometime after June 2015.

This is not the worst-case scenario from the VA and mental health, but this is my story. This can not continue, others are far worse off and need the help they ask for RIGHT NOW not months or even days later. Why is there not a program set up that's 24/7 hours where the Vet can come into the VA mental health building and be treated at that moment. I am going to school now so I hopefully can help another Vet with PTSD. I would like to work with in the VA, efficiently. They cannot continue on this path they are living up to the motto most vets live by now

"The VA giving Vets a second chance to die for their country"
The saddest part is it is the truth.
Sincerely,
Ret. US Army Vet
Alisa Hurkman

Like Alisa, I too have had the VA threaten to cancel my benefits for missing an appointment. The problem is that I knew I wasn't able to make the appointment and actively reached out to the VA, but could not get through to an actual person. So, I left a voicemail with my appointment details and that I needed to reschedule. I never heard anything until I received a letter reprimanding me for missing an appointment.

There's a common thread here: the need to be able to efficiently gain access to the right care in a *timely* and thorough manner. Nathan Lewis, a former Marine Corps Officer, shared this with me:

> After my transition from the Corps my wife suggested I seek help for my challenges related to my two tours in Iraq. I reached out to the local VA hospital and asked for support. I waited months for their response. After three or so months I contacted them again. I was given a list of items I had to complete. It was an admin exercise and I decided to seek help through the assistance of my private sector employer.

But what about those who cannot go outside of the VA for care? As a small business owner, I cannot afford private healthcare at this time. I am aware of several amazing psychologists in the DC area, but I simply cannot afford to pay for treatment out of pocket.

In conclusion, as a veteran seeking mental health treatment from the VA, my biggest issue is gaining timely access to the right type of treatment. For me, the barrier to this is on the VA's administrative side; gaining access to the right providers. I truly believe that streamlining this process and providing veterans with the appropriate mental health care will result in stronger families and dramatically reduce veteran unemployment and the tragic suicides that are plaguing the veteran community.

Mr. Chairman and members of the Committee, I wish to thank you for this opportunity to present my perspective today.

In: Veterans' Access to Mental Health Care ISBN: 978-1-63485-195-4
Editor: Edgar W. Schneider

Chapter 4

VETERANS HEALTH ADMINISTRATION: REVIEW OF VETERANS' ACCESS TO MENTAL HEALTH CARE*

VA Office of Inspector General

ACRONYMS AND ABBREVIATIONS

ARC	Allocation Resource Center
CBOC	Community Based Outpatient Clinic
CPT	Current Procedural Terminology
DSS	Decision Support System
Dx	Diagnosis
EBT	Evidence Based Psychotherapy
FTE	Full-Time Employee Equivalent
IOP	Intensive Outpatient Substance Use Treatment Program
Mgmt	Management
MH	Mental Health
OEF	Operation Enduring Freedom
OIF	Operation Iraqi Freedom
OIG	Office of Inspector General
OPES	Office of Productivity, Efficiency, and Staffing

* This is an edited, reformatted and augmented version of Report No. 12-00900-168, issued by the Department of Veterans Affairs, Office of Inspector General, April 23, 2012.

PAR	Performance and Accountability Report
PCT	Post-Traumatic Stress Disorder Clinical Team
PTSD	Post-Traumatic Stress Disorder
RVU	Relative Value Units
SUD	Substance Use Disorder
Tx	Treatment
VHA	Veterans Health Administration
VISN	Veterans Integrated Service Network
VistA	Veterans Health Information Systems and Technology Architecture
VSSC	Veterans Health Administration Support Service Center
WSDTT	Women's Stress Disorders Treatment Team
WVRU	Work Relative Value Units

EXECUTIVE SUMMARY

Results in Brief

The Office of Inspector General (OIG) conducted this review at the request of the Chairman and Ranking Member, U.S. Senate Committee on Veterans' Affairs, the Secretary of Veterans' Affairs, the Chairman and Ranking Member of the U.S. House Veterans' Affairs Committee and the Chairwoman and Ranking Member of the Subcommittee on Health, House Committee on Veterans' Affairs, after they expressed concerns that veterans may not be able to access the mental health care they need in a timely manner. The request asked the OIG to determine how accurately the Veterans Health Administration (VHA) records wait times for mental health services for both initial (new patients) and follow-up (established patients) visits and if the wait time data VA collects is an accurate depiction of the veteran's ability to access those services.

Background

VHA policy requires all first-time patients referred to or requesting mental health services receive an initial evaluation within 24 hours and a more comprehensive diagnostic and treatment planning evaluation within 14 days. The primary goal of the initial 24-hour evaluation is to identify patients with urgent care needs and to trigger hospitalization or the immediate initiation of outpatient care when needed. Primary care mental health providers, other referring licensed independent providers, or licensed independent mental health providers can conduct the initial 24-hour evaluation.

One method VHA uses to monitor access to mental health services is to calculate patients' waiting times by measuring the elapsed days from the desired dates of care to the dates of the treatment appointments. Medical facility schedulers must enter the correct desired dates of care in the system to ensure the accuracy of this measurement. VHA's goal is to see patients within 14 days of the desired dates of care.

VHA's Mental Health Performance Data Is Not Accurate or Reliable

VHA does not have a reliable and accurate method of determining whether they are providing patients timely access to mental health care services. VHA did not provide first-time patients with timely mental health evaluations and existing patients often waited more than 14 days past their desired date of care for their treatment appointment.

VHA's Measurement of a First-Time Patient's Access to a Full Mental Health Evaluation Was Not a Meaningful Measure of Waiting Time

In VA's FY 2011 Performance and Accountability Report (PAR), VHA reported 95 percent of first-time patients received a full mental health evaluation within 14 days. However, this measure had no real value as VHA measured how long it took VHA to conduct the evaluation, not how long the patient waited to receive an evaluation. For example, if a patient's primary care provider referred the patient to mental health service on September 15 and the medical facility scheduled and completed the evaluation on October 1, VHA's data showed the veteran waited 0-days for their evaluation. In reality, the veteran waited 15 days for their evaluation.

VHA's measurement differed from the defined objective of the measure that stated veterans should have further evaluation and initiation of mental health care in 14 days of a trigger encounter. VHA defined the trigger encounter as the veterans contact with the mental health clinic or the veteran's referral to the mental health service from another provider. VHA needs to redefine their measurement to ensure it meets the intent of the stated objective that is to make sure veterans receive a full mental health evaluation within 14 days.

VHA Was Not Providing All First-Time Patients a Full Mental Health Evaluation within 14 Days

Using the same data VHA used to calculate the 95 percent success rate shown in the FY 2011 PAR, we selected a statistical sample of completed evaluations to determine the starting and ending points of the elapsed day calculation. We conducted an independent assessment by reviewing patient records to review patients' visit dates, clinical notes, and consult records to identify the exact date of the trigger encounter (the date the patient initially contacted mental health seeking services, or when another provider referred the patient to mental health). We determined when the full evaluation containing a patient history, diagnosis, and treatment plan was completed. Based on our analysis of that information, we calculated the number of days between initial contact in mental health and the full mental health evaluation. Our analysis projected that VHA provided only 49 percent (approximately 184,000) of their evaluations within 14 days. On average, for the remaining patients, it took VHA about 50 days to provide them with their full evaluations.

VHA Overstated Its Success in Providing Veterans New and Follow-up Appointments for Treatment within 14 Days

VHA does not consider the full mental health evaluation as an appointment for treatment, but rather the evaluation is the prerequisite for VHA to develop a patient-appropriate treatment plan. Once VHA provides the patient with a full mental health evaluation, VHA schedules the patient for an appointment to begin treatment. We found that VHA did not always provide both new and established patients their appointments within 14 days of the patients' desired date—VHA's goal for timely patient access to care. VHA defines the desired date as the date on which the patient or the provider wants the patient to be seen without regard to schedule capacity. We reviewed patient records to identify the desired date (generally located in the physician's note as the date the patient needed to return to the clinic or shown as a referral from another provider) and calculated the elapsed days to the date of the patient's completed treatment appointment date. We projected nationwide that in FY 2011, VHA:

- Completed approximately 168,000 (64 percent) new patient appointments for treatment within 14 days of their desired date; thus, approximately 94,000 (36 percent) appointments nationwide exceeded 14 days. VHA data showed that 95 percent received timely care.
- Completed approximately 8.8 million (88 percent) follow-up appointments for treatment within 14 days of the desired date; thus, approximately 1.2 million (12 percent) appointments nationwide exceeded 14 days. Although we based our analysis on dates documented in VHA's medical records, we have less confidence in the integrity of this date because providers at three of the four medical centers we visited told us they requested a desired date of care based on their schedule availability. VHA data showed that 98 percent received timely care for treatment.

VHA Schedulers Did Not Consistently Follow Procedures

VHA schedulers were not following procedures outlined in VHA Directives, and, as a result, VHA's reported waiting time data was not accurate or reliable. For new patients, the scheduling clerks frequently stated they used the next available appointment slot as the desired appointment date for new patients. For established patients, medical providers told us they frequently scheduled the return to clinic appointments based on their known availability rather than the patient's clinical need. For example, providers may not have availability for 2–3 months, so they specify that as the return to clinic time frame.

OIG previously reported concerns with VHA's calculated wait time data in our *Audit of VHA's Outpatient Scheduling Procedures,* Report No. 04-02887-169, July 8, 2005 and *Audit of VHA's Outpatient Wait Times,* Report No. 07-00616-199, September 10, 2007. During both audits, OIG found that schedulers were entering an incorrect desired date. Given VHA's inability to correct this long-standing problem, VHA should reassess their training, competency, and oversight methods and develop appropriate controls to collect reliable and accurate appointment data.

Mental Health Staff Vacancies May Be Affecting VHA's Ability to Meet Timeliness Goals

According to VHA, from 2005 to 2010, mental health services increased their staff by 46 percent and treated 39 percent more patients. Despite the increase in mental health care providers, VHA's mental health care service staff still did not believe they had enough staff to handle the increased workload and consistently see patients within 14 days of the desired date.

In July 2011, the U.S. Senate Committee on Veterans' Affairs requested VA to conduct a survey that among other questions asked mental health professionals whether their medical center had adequate mental health staff to meet current veteran demands for care; 71 percent responded their medical center did not have adequate numbers of mental health staff. Based on our interviews at four medical centers, staff in charge of mental health services reported VHA's greatest challenge has been to hire and retain psychiatrists. Three of the four sites we visited had vacant psychiatry positions. We determined that a patient at the Salisbury VA Medical Center had to wait, on average, 86 days to see a psychiatrist. This was based on an analysis of VHA's data that identifies a provider's third next available appointment date for treatment. Staff at that facility told us they were still trying to replace three psychiatrists who left to go to a private practice in the past year. A comprehensive staffing analysis can help VHA determine if psychiatrist, or other mental health provider, vacancies are systemic issues impeding VHA's ability to meet mental health timeliness goals.

Measuring Access to VHA Mental Health Care

The data and measures needed by decision makers for effective planning and service provision may differ at the national, Veterans Integrated Service Network, and facility level. No measure of access is perfect or paints a complete picture in isolation. Meaningful analysis and decision making requires reliable data, on not only the timeliness of access but also on trends in demand for mental health services, treatments, and providers; the availability and mix of mental health staffing; provider productivity; and treatment capacity. These demand and supply variables in turn feedback upon a system's ability to provide treatment that is patient centered and timely.

VHA's 14-day follow-up measure provides decision makers with a limited picture of a new patient's ability to access and begin mental health treatment. Additionally, depending on a veteran's point of access, this metric does not truly measure VHA's stated objective "to ensure timely access for all veterans who are new to mental health." A series of timeliness and treatment engagement measures might provide decision makers with a more comprehensive view of the ability with which new patients can access mental health treatment. Furthermore, although VHA collects and reports mental health staffing and productivity data, the complexity of the computations and inaccuracies in some of the data sources, limits the usability of productivity information to fully assess current capacity, determine optimal resource distribution, evaluate productivity across the system, and establish mental health staffing and productivity standards.

Private sector entities with whom we spoke reported that their managers use multiple measures to assess a range of access parameters. These entities disseminate their dashboard reports to all levels of management thereby facilitating timely response to changing access dynamics. Beyond measures of timeliness (or delay) to mental health care, a dashboard of user friendly measures that incorporate aspects of patient demand, provider supply, clinic capacity, and provider productivity, anchored by a consistent set of business rules, might provide VHA decision makers with a more robust perspective from which to assess and timely respond to changes in access parameters.

Conclusion

VHA does not have a reliable and accurate method of determining whether they are providing patients timely access to mental health care services. VHA did not provide first-time patients with timely mental health evaluations and existing patients often waited more than 14 days past their desired date of care for their treatment appointment. As a result, performance measures used to report patient's access to mental health care do not depict the true picture of a patient's waiting time to see a mental health provider.

Although no measure of access is perfect or paints a complete picture in isolation, meaningful analysis and decision making requires reliable data, on not only the timeliness of access but also on trends in demand for mental health services, treatments, and providers; the availability and mix of mental health staffing; provider productivity; and treatment capacity. A series of timeliness and treatment engagement measures might provide decision makers with a more comprehensive view of the ability with which new patients can access mental health treatment.

Recommendations

1) We recommend the Under Secretary for Health revise the current full mental health evaluation measurement to ensure the measurement is

calculated to reflect the veteran's wait time experience upon contact with the mental health clinic or the veteran's referral to the mental health service from another provider to the completion of the evaluation.

2) We recommend the Under Secretary for Health reevaluate alternative measures or combinations of measures that could effectively and accurately reflect the patient experience of access to mental health appointments.
3) We recommend the Under Secretary for Health conduct a staffing analysis to determine if mental health staff vacancies represent a systemic issue impeding the Veterans Health Administration's ability to meet mental health timeliness goals, and if so, develop an action plan to correct the impediments.
4) We recommend the Under Secretary for Health ensure that data collection efforts related to mental health access are aligned with the operational needs of relevant decision makers throughout the organization.

Under Secretary for Health Comments

The Under Secretary for Health concurred with the OIG's findings and recommendations and stated VHA is unequivocally committed to providing Veterans the best care possible. The Under Secretary stated VHA would act rapidly on all findings that may improve Veterans' access to mental health care. (See Appendix E for the full text of the Under Secretary's comments.) We consider the planned actions acceptable and will follow up on the implementation.

LINDA A. HALLIDAY
Assistant Inspector General for Audits and Evaluations

JOHN D. DAIGH, JR., M.D.
Assistant Inspector General for Healthcare Inspections

INTRODUCTION

Purpose

The Chairman and Ranking Member of the U.S. Senate Committee on Veterans' Affairs, the Secretary of Veterans' Affairs, the Chairman and Ranking Member of the U.S. House Veterans' Affairs Committee and the Chairwoman and Ranking Member of the Subcommittee on Health, House Committee on Veteran's Affairs requested this review of veterans' access to mental health care. Specifically, they requested the Office of Inspector General (OIG) determine how accurately the Veterans Health Administration (VHA) records wait times for mental health (MH) for both initial (new patients) and follow-up (established patients) visits and if the wait time data VHA collects provides an accurate depiction of the veteran's ability to access those services.

BACKGROUND

VHA policy requires all new patients referred to or requesting mental health services receive an initial evaluation within 24 hours, and a more comprehensive diagnostic and treatment planning evaluation within 14 days. VHA's goal is to see patients within 14 days of the patient's desired date of care.

To ensure reliable waiting times, schedulers must input the correct desired date of care when creating appointments for treatment. According to VHA Directive 2010-027:

- For new patients, the patient defines the desired date without regard to schedule capacity. Once the desired date is established, schedulers must not alter the date to reflect an appointment date the patient acquiesces to accept for lack of appointment availability on the desired date.
- For established patients, the provider or scheduler will communicate a specific or a general time frame and the patient establishes the actual desired date. The scheduler is to offer and schedule an appointment on or as close to the desired date as possible. If there is a discrepancy between the patient and provider desired date, the scheduler must

contact the provider for a decision on the return appointment time frame.

VHA defines new patients as those who have not received care in a defined stop code or stop code group at that facility within the past 2 years; established patients represent all others. VHA measures the elapsed days from the desired dates of care to the dates of the appointments. Schedulers must enter the correct desired dates of care in the system to ensure the accuracy of this measurement.

RESULTS AND CONCLUSIONS

Issue 1: VHA's Mental Health Performance Data Is Not Accurate or Reliable

VHA's measurement of a first-time patient's access to a full mental health evaluation was not a meaningful measure to assess the time a veterans waits for a mental health appointment and VHA's performance data for mental health treatment appointments is not accurate or reliable. Our assessment showed VHA did not provide first-time patients with timely mental health evaluations and existing patients often waited more than 14 days past their desired dates of care for their treatment appointments. Based on our review, this occurred because VHA did not have an appropriate method in place to evaluate how well they were providing first-time patients a timely full mental health evaluation. Scheduling staff not following prescribed procedures, staffing shortages, and increasing workloads also contributed to inaccurate and unreliable data as well as delays in mental health care. As a result, VHA's leadership and decision makers' ability to make informed decisions for improving timely access to mental health care is constrained.

VHA's Mental Health Performance Data Is Not Accurate or Reliable

VHA does not have a reliable and accurate method of determining whether they are providing patients timely access to mental health care services. VHA did not provide first-time patients with timely mental health evaluations and existing patients often waited more than 14 days past their desired date of care for their treatment appointment.

VHA's Measurement of a First-Time Patient's Access to a Full Mental Health Evaluation Was Not a Meaningful Measure of Waiting Time

In VA's FY 2011 Performance and Accountability Report (PAR), VHA reported 95 percent of first-time patients received a full mental health evaluation within 14 days. However, this measure had no real value as VHA measured how long it took VHA to conduct the evaluation, not how long the patient waited to receive an evaluation. For example, if a patient's primary care provider referred the patient to mental health service on September 15 and the medical facility scheduled and completed the evaluation on October 1, VHA's data showed the veteran waited 0-days for their evaluation. In reality, the veteran waited 15 days for their evaluation.

VHA's measurement differed from the defined objective of the measure that stated veterans should have further evaluation and initiation of mental health care in 14 days of a trigger encounter. VHA Directive 2010-027 requires that all patients seeing a VA mental health provider for the first time receive a full evaluation within 14 days of either the patient's referral to mental health or the patient's self-contact seeking mental health services. According to VHA senior officials, a full evaluation consists of patient history, diagnosis, and treatment plan. According to VHA criteria, this measures the ability of VHA to ensure veterans new to mental health services will have initial mental health care and further evaluation in less than 15 days of either the patient's:

- Walk-in to the clinic or directly accessing mental health clinic staff through other means, such as telephone (referred to as a trigger encounter).
- Referral to mental health service from either the primary care provider or other specialty care provider.

VHA needs to redefine their measurement to ensure it meets the intent of the stated objective that is to make sure veterans receive a full mental health evaluation within 14 days.

OIG's Assessment of How Long Patients Waited to Receive a Full Mental Health Evaluation

Using the same data VHA used to calculate the 95 percent success rate shown in the FY 2011 PAR, we selected a statistical sample of completed evaluations to determine the starting and ending points of the elapsed day calculation. Specifically, we reviewed patient records and used information in

VHA's Compensation and Pension Records Interchange to review patients' visit dates, clinical notes, and consult records to identify when the patient initially contacted mental health seeking services or when another provider referred the patient to mental health. We determined if the full evaluation contained patient history, diagnosis, and treatment plan. Based on that information, we calculated the number of days between initial contact in mental health and the full mental health evaluation. Our analysis projected that VHA provided only 49 percent (approximately 184,000) of first-time patients their evaluation within 14 days. On average, for the remaining patients, it took VHA about 50 days to provide them with their full evaluations.

OIG's Site Visits to Four VHA Medical Centers

We visited four medical centers to evaluate their processes of scheduling first-time patients for mental health care. All four medical centers had a process in place to conduct an initial assessment within 24 hours to comply with VHA directives and ensure the patient was not in immediate risk. At that point, the scheduling processes varied, as highlighted in the procedures identified below.

- The Spokane VA Medical Center established an intake clinic staffed by multiple providers consisting of social workers and psychologists. The clinic contacted patients within 24 hours and scheduled them for a full evaluation within 14 days. Clinic staff uses the 24-hour contact process to assess whether the veteran is in an immediate danger. If there is an emergency, the inpatient psychiatrists handle the intervention with the patient. Following the full evaluation, an intake committee, consisting of social workers, psychologists, and psychiatrists, meets every Tuesday and Thursday to discuss if the recommended treatment plan is appropriate. Because psychiatrists are in short supply, this process appears to make the best use of staff.
- The Salisbury VA Medical Center used a telephone triage system to contact the patient and assess the urgency of their condition. This triage (Current Procedural Terminology (CPT) code 98968) qualifies as a full evaluation because the triage performed collects a brief history, diagnosis, and treatment plan to follow up with a provider in the future. However, in discussions with triage staff, we found that this procedure consisted of talking to the veteran for at least 21 minutes using a template with a list of questions. The telephone triage staff would schedule the patient for their intake appointment, and this

was usually at least 3 months in the future. The telephone triage staff stated that although VHA considers this effort a full evaluation and records it as such under CPT code 98968. They agreed that in 21 minutes they could only provide a minimum evaluation.

VHA Overstated Its Performance Outcomes to Provide Veterans New and Follow-up Appointments for Treatment within 14 Days

Once VHA provides the patient with a full mental health evaluation, VHA schedules the patient for an appointment to begin treatment. VHA does not consider the full mental health evaluation as an appointment for treatment, but rather the evaluation is the prerequisite for VHA to develop a patient-appropriate treatment plan. VHA did not always provide patients their appointments within 14 days of the patients' desired dates— VHA's goal for timely patient access to care. Desired date is the date on which the patient or the provider wants the patient to be seen without regard to schedule capacity.

OIG's Assessment of How Long Patients Waited for their Mental Health Care Treatment Appointment

For treatment appointments of patients new to a specific mental health clinic, as prescribed by VHA Directives and training modules, we used the date a provider referred the patient to the clinic as the desired date. For example, a physician treating a patient in a substance abuse clinic determines the patient needs treatment for depression and on July 1 refers the patient to an appropriate clinic specializing in treating depression. We used July 1 as the desired date. When we could not identify a consult referral date, we used the appointment creation date as the desired date. In FY 2011, we projected nationwide that VHA completed approximately 168,000 (64 percent) new patient appointments within 14 days of their desired date; thus, approximately 94,000 (36 percent) appointments nationwide exceeded 14 days. VHA data showed that 95 percent received timely care.

For follow-up treatment appointments, we used the date the provider requested for the patient's return to the clinic. Although we based our analysis on dates documented in VHA's medical records, we have less confidence in the integrity of this date, because providers at three of the four medical centers we visited told us they requested a desired date of care based on their schedule availability. For example, if they knew they could not see the patient for another 2–3 months, they scheduled the patient's return to clinic in that time frame to align with their availability. VHA completed approximately 8.8 million (88 percent) follow-up appointments within 14 days of the desired date; thus, almost 1.2 million (12 percent) appointments nationwide exceeded 14 days. VHA data showed that 98 percent received timely care.

VHA's National Access List

VHA uses the national access list to monitor access and identify delays in mental health care. As of January 2012, VHA's national access list, which included both first-time patients and patients receiving follow-up appointments for treatment, reported about 15,000 mental health care appointments that exceeded VHA's standard of scheduling appointments within 14 days of their desired date. Approximately 12,600 (84 percent) appointments were scheduled from 15 to 60 days, and approximately 2,400 (16 percent) of the appointments were scheduled more than 60 days, from the patient's desired appointment date. We did not validate the completeness or accuracy of this list.

Next Available Appointment

VHA captures data to determine the number of days until the third next available treatment appointment for specific clinics. Calculating the wait time to the third next available appointment is a common practice for assessing a provider's ability to see patients in a timely manner. According to VHA data, the number of completed appointments in mental health clinics during FY 2011 was about 10.3 million with 7.3 million (71 percent) of these showing the third next available appointment was within 14 days. In other words, in FY 2011, VHA generally had the capacity to schedule 71 percent of their patients within 14 days.

Determining the wait time to the third next available appointment is not an absolute measure of VHA's ability to provide timely access (an appointment within 14 days) because there are two available appointment times prior to the third next available appointment that clinics can use to schedule patients. However, in July 2011, the U.S. Senate Committee on Veterans' Affairs requested VA to conduct a survey that among other questions asked mental health professionals whether they could schedule a patient appointment within 14 days in their own mental health clinics. Of the respondents, 63 percent said they could schedule a new patient appointment, and 61 percent said they could schedule an established patient appointment within 14 days. The survey appears to corroborate VHA's data of the third next available appointment.

Scheduling Procedures Were Not Followed

VHA schedulers were not following procedures outlined in VHA Directives and, as a result, VHA's reported waiting time data was not accurate or reliable. For new patients, the scheduling clerks frequently stated they used the next available appointment slot as the desired appointment date for new patients. Even though a consult referral, or contact from the veteran requesting care, may have been submitted weeks or months earlier than the patient's appointment date, the desired appointment date was determined by and recorded as the next available appointment date. For established patients, medical providers told us they frequently scheduled the return to clinic date based on their known availability rather than the patient's clinical need. For example, providers may not have availability for 2–3 months, so they specify that as the return to clinic time frame.

Using inappropriate and inconsistent scheduling practices greatly distorts the actual waiting time for appointments. We analyzed VHA's data and found that:

- Of the new patient treatment appointments, VHA staff scheduled 81 percent (211,000) on the patient's desired date of care resulting in a 0-day wait.
- Of the established patient treatment appointments, VHA staff scheduled 88 percent (8.9 million) on the patient's desired date of care resulting in a 0-day wait.

Based on discussions with medical center staff and our review of data, we contend it is not plausible to have that many appointments scheduled on the exact day the patient requested. In our opinion, this data reflects inappropriate scheduling practices and it is not representative of how long the patient waited to receive care.

OIG previously reported concerns with VHA's calculated wait time data in our *Audit of VHA's Outpatient Scheduling Procedures,* Report No. 04-02887-169, July 8, 2005 and *Audit of VHA's Outpatient Wait Times,* Report No. 07-00616-199, September 10, 2007. During both audits, OIG found that schedulers were entering an incorrect desired date. VHA Directives require all scheduling staff to complete training on scheduling procedures and require VA Medical Center directors to:

- Ensure every scheduler successfully completes all training modules.
- Ensure all schedulers receive an annual competency assessment.
- Ensure completion of an annual scheduler audit of the timeliness and appropriateness of scheduling actions, and the accuracy of desired dates.

- Be vigilant in the identification and avoidance of inappropriate scheduling activities.

Our review did not fully analyze if the construct of VHA's training and oversight program contributed to the problems we identified. Regardless, given VHA's inability to correct this long-standing problem, VHA should reassess their training, competency, and oversight methods to ensure reliable and accurate appointment data is captured.

Increasing Workload and Staffing Shortages

According to VHA, from 2005 to 2010, mental health services increased their staff by 46 percent and treated 39 percent more patients. Despite the increase in mental health care providers, VHA's mental health care service staff still did not believe they had enough staff to handle the increased workload and consistently see patients within 14 days of the desired dates.

The VA survey asked mental health professionals whether their medical center had adequate mental health staff to meet current veteran demands for care; 71 percent responded their medical center did not have adequate numbers of mental health staff. Based on our interviews at four medical centers, staff in charge of mental health services reported VHA's greatest challenge has been to hire and retain psychiatrists. We analyzed access to psychiatrists at the four medical centers we visited by determining how long a patient would have to wait for the physician's third available appointment. On average, a patient had to wait 41 days. Specifically:

- 19 days at the Denver VA Medical Center
- 28 days at the Milwaukee VA Medical Center
- 80 days at the Spokane VA Medical Center
- 86 days at the Salisbury VA Medical Center

Three of the four sites we visited had vacant psychiatry positions. The Salisbury VA Medical Center had an average wait of 86 days for the psychiatrists' third next available appointment. Staff at that facility told us they lost three psychiatrists to private practice facilities in the past year. VHA needs to conduct a staffing analysis to determine if psychiatrist, or other mental health provider, vacancies are systemic issues impeding VHA's ability to meet mental health timeliness goals.

Conclusion

Most first-time patients waited more than 14 days for their full mental health evaluation and VHA could not always provide existing patients their treatment appointments within 14 days of their desired dates. Performance measure data for mental health appointments was not accurate or reliable. Without accurate and appropriate data, VHA's leadership and decision makers cannot make informed decisions for improving access to mental health care.

Recommendations

1) We recommend the Under Secretary for Health revise the current full mental health evaluation measurement to ensure the measurement is calculated to reflect the veteran's wait time experience upon contact with the mental health clinic or the veteran's referral to the mental health service from another provider to the completion of the evaluation.
2) We recommend the Under Secretary for Health reevaluate alternative measures or combinations of measures that could effectively and accurately reflect the patient experience of access to mental health appointments.
3) We recommend the Under Secretary for Health conduct a staffing analysis to determine if mental health staff vacancies represent a systemic issue impeding the Veterans Health Administration's ability to meet mental health timeliness goals, and if so, develop an action plan to correct the impediments.

Under Secretary for Health Comments

The Under Secretary for Health concurred with the OIG's findings and recommendations. VHA has convened a work group to examine how best to measure wait time and develop an action plan to create new metrics. They are committed to developing measures that will reliably and accurately capture appointment scheduling performance for new and ongoing treatment. VHA began collecting vacancy data for mental health staff on January 31, 2012, and will assess the impact of vacancies on operations and develop recommendations for improvement. We consider the planned actions acceptable and will follow up on the implementation.

The Under Secretary for Health provided the following technical comments. The Under Secretary stated that the metric labeled in the report as "First-Time Patient's Access to a Full Mental Health Evaluation," was never intended to measure waiting time, but rather, as the OIG suggests, it was intended to measure how long it took VHA to conduct the evaluation. The Under Secretary also stated that the OIG did not use VHA's methodology of the desired date to assess the accuracy of the metric for new patient waiting time. Rather, OIG assessed waiting time based on the time the appointment was entered into the system, which was the create date.

OIG Response to VHA's Technical Comments

The OIG does not agree that the metric was intended to measure how long it took VHA to conduct the evaluation. The metric states that veterans defined as new to mental health will have further evaluation and initiation of mental health care in less than 15 days of trigger encounter (walk in or direct access to mental health clinic) or a referral to mental health service from either primary care provider or other specialty care provider. Therefore, we believe VHA should be measuring the time from when the patient directly contacts mental health service or the initial consult referral from a primary or specialty care provider.

We used the premise that new patients want to be seen as soon as possible to assess the accuracy of the metric for new patient waiting time. For appointments with a consult referral we used the referral date as the desired date. For appointments without a consult referral we used the appointment create date as the desired date since that was the earliest date indicating the veteran wanted mental health care.

Issue 2: VHA Measures Do Not Fully Reflect Critical Dimensions of Mental Health Care Access

VHA's primary mental health access measure, the 14-day follow-up measure, provides decision makers with a limited picture of a new patient's ability to access and begin mental health treatment at VA. Additionally, depending on a veteran's point of access, it may not truly measure VHA's objective "to ensure timely access for all veterans who are new to mental health." A series of timeliness and treatment engagement measures that better reflect the various dimensions of access may provide VHA decision makers with a more comprehensive view of the ability with which new patients can access mental health treatment. Developing strong access measures not only requires an understanding of how veterans access and demand mental health services but also what VA's supply and availability is for services.

Defining Access

In its 1993 report on Access to Health Care in America, the Institute of Medicine defined access as the timely use of personal health services to achieve the best possible outcomes. The authors noted their definition forces one to identify those areas of medical care in which services can be shown to influence health status and then to ask whether the relatively poorer outcomes of some population groups can be explained by problems related to access. The Institute of Medicine definition also emphasized the need to go beyond typical approaches relying mainly on enumerating health care providers, the uninsured, or encounters with health care providers to identify access problems. The authors also commented, "no matter how generally efficacious a particular health service may be, a good outcome cannot always be guaranteed. The most important consideration is whether people have an opportunity for a good outcome—especially in those instances in which medical care can make a difference."[1]

Access to mental health care is a multi-dimensional concept that can be assessed relative to a variety of domains including:

- Geographic location (travel time, distance)
- Temporal (time to appointments, waiting time, time of day, day of week)
- Setting (primary care versus mental health, general mental health care versus specialized mental health care)
- Urgency (emergency mental health treatment, routine treatment)
- Type of mental health service (medication management, psychotherapy, case management, group versus individual treatment)
- Provider (psychiatrist, psychologist, social worker, nurse practitioner, addictions counselor)
- Subjective consumer satisfaction
- Affordability[2] and utilization (number of encounters)
- Penetrance (percent of at-risk patients receiving treatment)

Overview and Definition of VHA Mental Health Access Measures

At the November 30, 2011, Senate Committee on Veterans' Affairs hearing, "VA Mental Health Care: Addressing Wait Times and Access to Care," VHA reported that to address mental health access, a new four-part mental health measure would be included in the performance contract for VHA leadership. The measures in the performance contract would define what leadership is accountable to accomplish. Accordingly, in the FY 2012 Network Director Performance Plans, one of the items used to evaluate the performance of Veterans Integrated Service Network (VISN) Directors is "the Network Director assures timely and appropriate access to mental health services." The four measures referred to at the hearing are incorporated in the FY 2012 performances measures listed for this element. The performance plan includes a fifth measure based on desired date. The limitations of the desired date measure were discussed in an earlier section of this report. Table 1 includes an explanation of the numerator and denominator used for the four referenced measures. The four measures are:

1) Percentage of eligible patient evaluations documented within 14 days of new mental health patient index encounter
2) Mental health follow-up within 7 days of discharge from an inpatient mental health unit
3) Percentage of Operation Enduring Freedom/Operation Iraqi Freedom (OEF/OIF) veterans with a new diagnosis of post-traumatic stress disorder (PTSD), receiving eight therapy visits within a 14-week period within 1 year of the initial mental health visit
4) Percentage of patients with an activated suicide high-risk flag placed on charts who receive four follow-up visits within a 4-week period following inpatient hospital discharge

Points of Access and Flow of Veterans With PTSD and Substance Use Disorder through VHA

Understanding how patients might access and move through VHA care provides a framework from which to construct meaningful access measures. The discussion that follows illustrates that in isolation, the first measure (14-day follow-up for new patients), provides decision makers with a limited picture of a new patient's ability to access and begin mental health treatment. A series of timeliness and treatment engagement measures might provide decision makers with a more comprehensive view of the ability with which new patients can access mental health treatment. Additionally, on closer review we found that depending on a veteran's point of access, measure 1 does not truly measure VHA's stated objective "to ensure timely access for all veterans who are new to mental health."

Table 1. Measures/Monitors Used by VHA To Monitor Access to Mental Health Care

Measure	Numerator	Denominator
1. Percentage of eligible patient encounters documented within 14 days of new mental health patient index encounter (14-day follow-up for new patients)	Veterans with encounter in specific mental health stops with a full evaluation < 15 days from date of initial trigger encounter or referral (consult).3	Veterans with encounters in any stop code except compensation and pension, neuropsychological testing and smoking cessation for a mental health diagnosis /problem and no prior encounters in specific mental health stops in the previous 24 months at that specific medical center. Veterans with a Mental health diagnosis who are treated in Primary Care and not referred to mental health are not in this monitor.
2. Mental health Inpatient 7 day follow-up (7-day follow-up discharge)	Mental health discharges with a faceto-face, telehealth, or telephone encounter in a mental health stop code during the 7 days after discharge. The initial follow up encounter cannot be on the same day as the discharge from inpatient. If initial follow-up contact is by telephone within 7 days, a face-to-face or telemental health follow up must occur within 14 days.	VA inpatient discharges in which the patient had at least 1 bed day of care on a mental health service.

Table 1. (Continued)

Measure	Numerator	Denominator
3. OEF/OIF veterans with 8 psychotherapy visits in 14 weeks (OEF/OIF Psychotherapy)	Those patients are then required to have 8 psychotherapy sessions (using the CPT codes 90801, 90806, 90807, 90808, 90809, 90818, 90819, 90821, 90822, 90853) within 14 weeks of one another sometime during that FY.	Operation Enduring Freedom/Operation Iraqi Freedom (OEF/OIF) veterans who have primary PTSD diagnoses in two separate outpatient encounters are included in the denominator during the month of their second diagnoses.
4. High-risk suicide monitor (High Risk for suicide)	Total number of patients flagged as Suicide High Risk at discharge that received a qualifying follow-up mental health encounter with a specific provider Person Class in each of 4 weeks following discharge.4	Total number of patients with the health factor "Suicide High Risk PRF Placed on Chart" activated. Activation can be in either in or outpatient setting.

Source: Table is from VA OIG. Numerators and Denominators are from VHA VSSC website.

Further, meaningful analysis and decision making requires reliable data on not only the timeliness of access but also on trends in demand for mental health services, treatments, and providers; the availability and mix of mental health staffing; provider productivity; and long-term treatment capacity. These demand and supply variables in turn feedback upon a system's ability to provide treatment that is patient centered and timely.

To understand access measures within the broader context of VHA mental health care, it is important to understand how a patient may access and move through VHA care. In this section, we describe a qualitative model of flow into VHA care for patients with a PTSD diagnosis (Figure 1) and depict a model of flow through VHA for patients with PTSD and patients with a substance use disorder (Figures 2 and 3). These models illustrate that VHA care has multiple access points and that demand for care is dynamic. At a given point in time, not all patients who need care seek it, and of those patients who seek care, not all continue care.

Flow of Veterans with PTSD

Figure 1 depicts the demand for VHA PTSD care. VHA's U.S. Vets database is a list of all veterans in the United States regardless of whether or not they have accessed or utilized VA care or benefits. Within the U.S. Vets population, some veterans may have been diagnosed with PTSD while in the military. Other veterans in the population may not have PTSD, did not display symptoms of PTSD while in the military, or were not diagnosed with PTSD during their military service.

Of those diagnosed with PTSD in the Department of Defense, some veterans do not seek mental health care after leaving the military (for example, those treated in Department of Defense with resolution of symptoms or veterans not seeking care due to stigma related concerns); some veterans seek care in the private, community mental health, or alternative public sectors (such as through Tricare); some veterans seek care through VHA; and others may initially seek care elsewhere and then through VHA at a later point in time.

Of those without a Department of Defense (DOD) PTSD diagnosis, some veterans are not in need of mental health care after leaving the military; some develop PTSD symptoms and seek care through private, community, or alternative public sector sources; some seek care through VHA for non-mental health-related conditions, and a sub-set of these veterans may subsequently develop PTSD symptoms; while other veterans develop PTSD symptoms and initially seek care through VHA for this condition. Figure 1, depicts the flow of patients with a PTSD diagnosis (indicated by Dx) into VHA. The green box and green arrow toward the bottom of the figure are used to represent the demand for PTSD evaluation and treatment within VHA.

Of note, the demand at a given VHA health care facility is dynamic and may fluctuate in relation to trends not only in the percentage of patients already within VHA care that need and/or seek mental health treatment at that location but to trends in the number of veterans who develop or initiate access to treatment within VHA for mental health-related conditions.

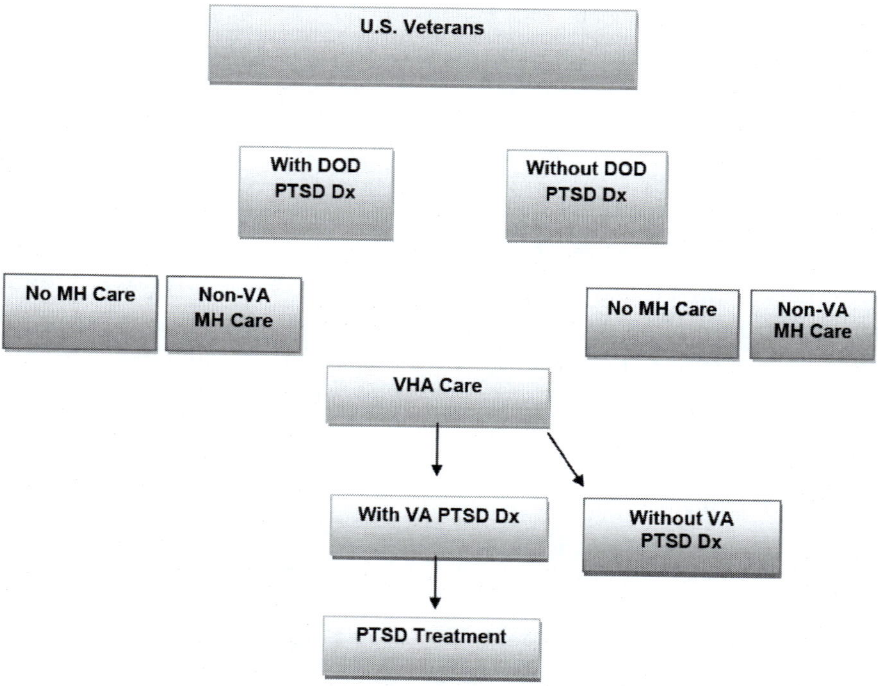

Figure 1. DEMAND=f(x) POPULATION, PTSD BURDEN, PTSD Dx.

Not all patients in need of mental health treatment seek treatment. Some patients seek or are referred to care but do not keep appointments. Other patients may enter into care but are difficult to engage in sustained treatment. Timely entry into treatment and the receipt of services can influence the quality of mental health and substance use services.

Measure 1: 14-Day Follow-Up (New Patients)

A 2005 study of referrals to the Johns Hopkins Bayview Medical Center community psychiatry adult and child/adolescent outpatient programs from 1995 to 2000 found increased wait times for an initial appointment for services at a community mental health center adversely affected the rate of kept appointments. In their clinic population, the study's authors found a linear relationship between appointment delay and cancelations and no-shows. The rate of cancelations and no-shows was 12 percent for patients who were given an appointment on the same day as the initial contact and 23 percent for the patients who were given an appointment the day after the initial contact. The rate rose to 42 percent among the patients whose appointments were 7 days after initial contact and reached a maximum of 44 percent among patients for whom the initial appointments were 13 days following initial contacts. Of note, the effect of wait time to initial mental health appointment might differ in other clinics where the patient population characteristics differ from the population in the community mental health center utilized in the study.[5]

A 2011 study examined the impact of days to treatment admission on the probability of completing four sessions of care within outpatient addiction treatment program units funded by the Network for the Improvement of Addiction Treatment. Data was analyzed for a cohort of patients from October 2003 to December 2004 and a second cohort of patients from January 2005 to March 2006. The study findings demonstrated a strong decrement in the probability of completing four sessions of treatment with increasing time between the clinical assessment and first treatment session.[6] These studies suggest that the motivation to show for and engage in mental health evaluation in treatment may wane as the delay between referral and receipt of initial evaluation and treatment increases.

VHA Handbook 1160.01, *Uniform Mental Health Services in VA Medical Centers and Clinics,* states that evaluations and treatment for mental health conditions can be provided through primary care and other medical settings or by arrangements with non-VA community services. New patients requesting or referred for mental health services must receive an initial evaluation within 24 hours and a more comprehensive diagnostic and treatment planning evaluation within 14 days. The primary goal of the initial 24-hour evaluation is to identify patients with urgent care needs and to trigger hospitalization or the immediate initiation of outpatient care when needed. The initial 24-hour evaluation can be conducted by primary care, mental health providers, other referring licensed independent providers, or by licensed independent mental health providers.[7]

The Deputy Undersecretary for Health for Operations and Management's Monitors and Guidelines for FY 2010 included what we refer to in this report as measure 1 within the domain of access. The monitor was titled "ensure timely access for all new veterans who need mental health care." According to VHA monitor documentation, the objective of measure 1 is to ensure timely access for all veterans who are new to mental health. Veterans defined as new to mental health will have further evaluation and the initiation of mental health care will occur within 15 days of a trigger encounter (walk in or direct access to mental health clinic) or a referral to mental health service from either primary care provider or other specialty care provider.[8]

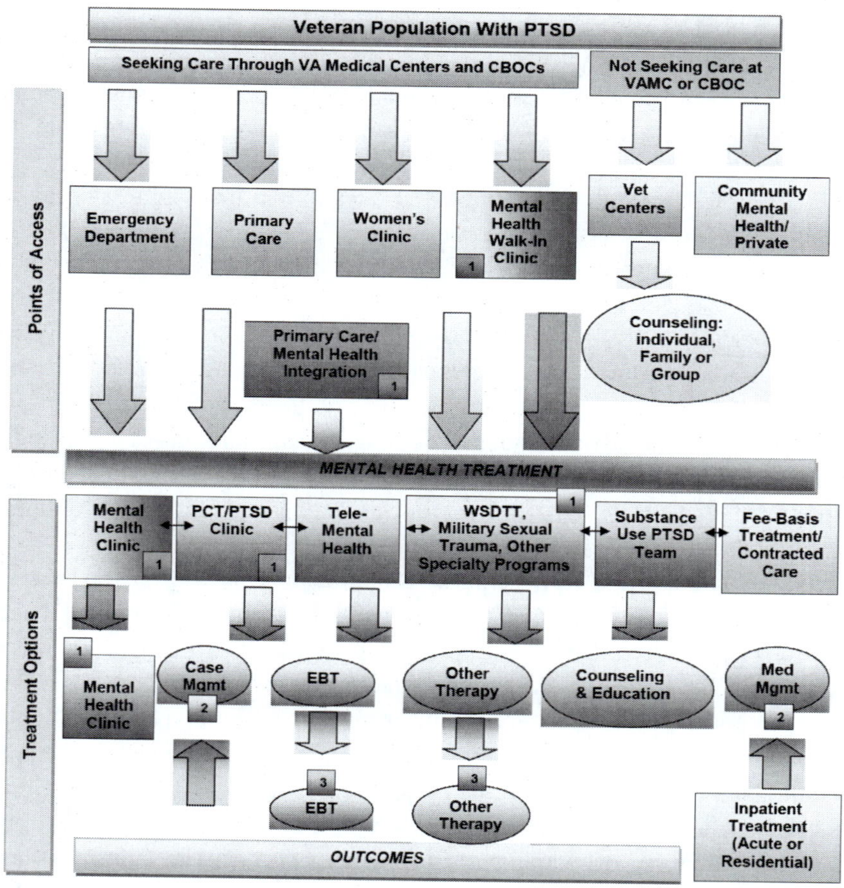

Source: VA OIG.

Figure 2. Flow of Patients with PTSD.

In practice, how VHA collects and reports data for measure 1 differs in part from the objective described for the measure. The trigger for measure 1 is not usually a referral or consult. Instead, it is typically an initial visit at a mental health clinic 500 series stop code. This distinction is illustrated in Figure 2, which represents the flow of patients with PTSD symptoms through possible VHA outpatient treatment settings, toward possible treatment options in primary care and specialty mental health treatment venues. Not all specialized mental health clinics depicted in the diagram are located at each VHA site, such as a women's stress disorders treatment team (WSDTT), military sexual trauma clinic, or substance use PTSD treatment team clinic.

Alternative paths that trigger measure 1 are depicted in Figure 2. (See Appendix D for detailed legend of Figure 2.) The data underlying measure 1 informs decision makers regarding the timeliness within which comprehensive new patient evaluations are completed but not necessarily the timeliness within which patients requesting or referred for mental health services receive a comprehensive evaluation or treatment.

As is apparent in Figure 2, there is not one uniform route or channel toward treatment for all patients but multiple potential channels through which patients may access evaluation and PTSD care and by which measure 1 will or will not be triggered:

1) Patients may utilize VHA primary care services but may seek mental health treatment outside of VHA through a private or community provider.
2) Patients may not seek or may decline PTSD treatment at the medical center or Community Based Outpatient Clinic (CBOC) but may seek counseling at a readjustment-counseling center (Vet Center). Evaluation at a vet center is not captured in measure 1.
3) Patients triaged in a primary care or mental health clinic may, under certain circumstances, be referred outside of VHA for treatment by a fee basis provider. Unless the fee basis provider treats patients on VA facility grounds, the time to completed evaluation is not captured in measure 1 for fee basis treatment.
4) Patients with PTSD symptoms may initially be screened and evaluated by a primary care provider in a primary care clinic or a comprehensive women's clinic in those facilities that have a women's clinic. Patients evaluated in these settings may decline referral to mental health and opt to be treated for PTSD symptoms by their

primary care provider. These patients would not be captured by measure 1.

5) Patients presenting to a primary care or other medical clinic with PTSD symptoms may be referred to a specialized mental health primary care-mental health integration clinic provider who is co-located and or/collaborates with the patient's primary care provider. An integrated primary care-mental health visit is captured by the decision support system (DSS) stop code/identifier 534. If the patient was seen for comprehensive evaluation by the mental health clinician on the same day, the visit would be picked up by measure 1 as a 0 day wait. If a comprehensive evaluation cannot be completed by a primary care-mental health integrated clinic provider on that day, then the measure captures the time from the index primary care- mental health integrated clinic provider visit to the time of the next visit with a primary care-mental health integrated clinic provider at which the evaluation is completed.
6) If a patient is seen in a primary care clinic, another non-mental health medical clinic, or the emergency department and a referral is made for a mental health appointment at a specialized mental health clinic, for example mental health clinic or PTSD Clinical Team (PCT) clinic, the clock for measure 1 is not triggered until evaluation is initiated on the day the patient presents at the mental health clinic for the appointment. If a comprehensive evaluation was completed within the index visit to the mental health clinic, this would be captured as a 0 day wait. If the evaluation is completed at a subsequent visit, then the time from the initial visit to the subsequent visit is captured by the measure.
7) If a patient calls PCT or another mental health clinic directly and sets up an appointment, again, the clock for measure 1 begins on the day of presentation (not when the appointment is requested) at the clinic, and the clock stops on the day a comprehensive evaluation is completed. If the evaluation was completed on the day of an initial trigger presentation, this would be captured as a 0 day wait. If the patient receives a triage evaluation at the initial visit, then the clock for measure 1 begins with the initial mental health visit and ends when evaluation is completed at a subsequent mental health clinic or PCT visit.
8) If a new patient spontaneously presents to a mental health walk-in clinic and a comprehensive evaluation is completed on the same day,

this would be captured by measure 1 as having a zero day wait. A new patient spontaneously presenting to a walk-in clinic that receives an initial or triage evaluation and is scheduled for evaluation in another mental health clinic would trigger measure 1 at the time of presentation to the walk-in clinic. In this scenario, measure 1 would capture the time from the walk-in clinic visit to the day of completion of evaluation in the second mental health clinic.

9) While measure 1 provides information regarding completion of new patient evaluations within 14 days of an index mental health encounter, it does not capture the timeliness within which new patients are evaluated and treated from when they are initially referred or initially request an appointment. In addition, it would not capture the timeliness with which established patients are seen for a second, third, or subsequent mental health appointments.
10) Once a comprehensive evaluation is completed in a specialized mental health clinic, referral to a different specialized mental health clinic would not be captured in measure 1. For example, if a patient is evaluated and treated in a general mental health clinic for PTSD but is referred to in an intensive outpatient substance use treatment program (IOP) during the course of their treatment in the mental health clinic, the wait time from referral by the mental health clinic to treatment in the IOP clinic is not captured by measure 1 or another measure. The completion of an evaluation starting and ending during the initial or a subsequent visit to the PCT clinic would also not be captured in the measure because the patient is not new to mental health.
11) Access to specific mental health providers (psychiatrist, psychologist, social worker, nurse practitioner, substance use counselor) may vary by VHA site. Timeliness measures in isolation would not capture access to specific providers for which staffing, capacity, and productivity data would be informative.

Measure 2: 7-Day Follow-Up Discharge

The weeks following discharge from inpatient mental health hospitalization represent a period of increased suicide risk. A British study found that patients receiving closer follow-up and more intensive aftercare were less likely to commit suicide.[9,10] A large Danish study found two sharp peaks for suicide around psychiatric hospitalization—one in the first week after admission and another in the first week after discharge.[11]

Measure 2 (follow-up within 7 days post hospitalization) is depicted in Figure 2. For measure 2, the clock for the measure begins when a discharge is entered into the system and ends when a face-to-face, telehealth, or telephone encounter is completed. The OIG will be collecting information related to measure 2 as part of the onsite Combined Assessment Program review process during the spring 2012 Combined Assessment Program cycle.

Measure 3: OEF/OIF Veterans with Eight Psychotherapy Visits in 14 Weeks

Access to specific mental health treatment services including medication management, case management, individual or group evidence-based psychotherapy (EBT) for PTSD, other therapies (such as supportive therapy), and counseling and educational groups, may differ at each VHA site (such as a VA Medical Center or CBOC). The occurrence and duration of therapy appointments can be captured with CPT codes, but the content of the therapy provided, whether it is a form of EBT (such as cognitive behavioral therapy) or another type of therapy (such as supportive therapy), cannot be captured by existing administrative codes. Measure 3 (OEF/OIF veterans with a new diagnosis of PTSD, receiving eight therapy visits within a 14-week period within 1 year of the initial mental health visit), is used by VHA as an indirect marker of whether new OEF/OIF patients are receiving a course of evidence-based therapy (a specific mental health treatment).

While the intent of the measure appears sound, upon review of recent data for this measure we noted that totals of veterans meeting the measure for certain VISNs exceeded the national total, and the variation among VISNs was very wide. The Office of Mental Health Service explained these discrepancies by noting that data extraction techniques for the measure were still being refined in order to resolve counting effects of patients receiving therapy in overlapping 14-week periods and fiscal years.

Measure 4: High-Risk Suicide Monitor

Measure 4, which requires four follow-up visits in 4 weeks following discharge for patients flagged as high risk, is not depicted in Figure 2 but would be represented in a fashion similar to that shown for measure 3 with an arrow initially emanating from inpatient care. The OIG will be collecting information related to measure 4 as part of the on-site Combined Assessment Program review process during the Spring 2012 Combined Assessment Program cycle.

Flow of Veterans with Substance Use Disorders through VHA

Figure 3 depicts the multi-channel flow of patients with substance use issues through possible VHA treatment settings, toward possible treatment options in primary care and specialty mental health treatment venues. The conventions are similar to those used in Figure 2. The complexity of flow is heightened by the potential need for inpatient or outpatient detoxification, residential versus outpatient rehabilitation and recovery treatment, and relapse potential.

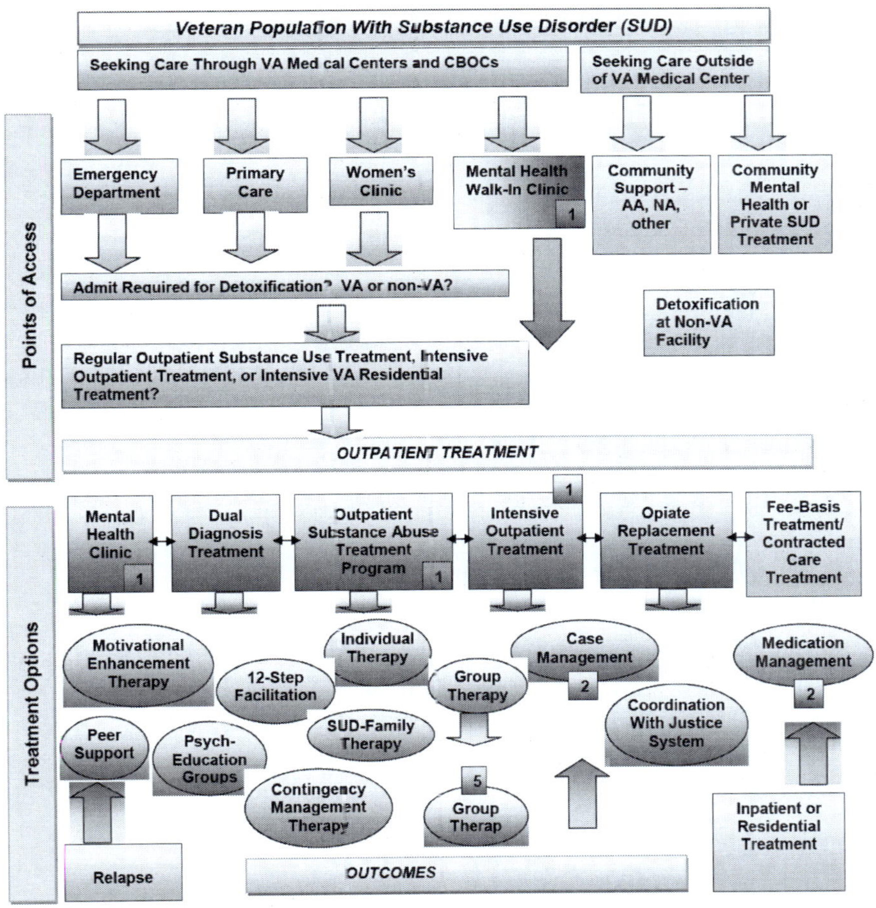

Source: VA OIG.

Figure 3. Flow of Patients with SUD.

As in Figure 2, the small squares containing a number 1 and a number 2 refer to measures 1 and 2. The small square containing a number 5 is used to depict a VHA monitor that captures the percent of patients beginning a new episode of treatment for substance use disorder who maintain continuous treatment involvement for at least 90 days as demonstrated by at least 2 days with visits every 30 days for a total of 90 days in any outpatient specialty substance use clinic. This is a measure of treatment engagement. As with patients with PTSD, there are multiple points of access and measure 1 invariably reflects access contingent on the patient's point of entry into treatment.

Bundled and Competing Access Measures

The data and measures needed by decision makers for planning and service provision may differ at the national, VISN, and facility level. No measure is perfect or paints a complete picture in isolation.

A bundle of related timeliness measures, if feasible, might include a measure of time from referral, no matter where a patient presents (by self or by primary care or other medical provider), to initial triage evaluation (time $t_0 - t_1$); time from initial evaluation to completed comprehensive evaluation (time $t_1 – t_2$); time from the date of completed evaluation to the next treatment appointment (time $t_2 – t_3$) or from the initial evaluation to initiation of treatment (t_1-t_3); an engagement measure (percentage of patients seen a threshold number of times during the first t_x days of treatment, such as 45 days), and a measure from time of referral by one specialized mental health clinic (such as General Mental Health) to other select specialized mental health clinics (for example, PCT or IOP).

Beyond measure of timeliness (or delay) to mental health care, a composite or family of measures to broadly inform access might also include: (1) provider panel size; (2) a measure of demand for services; (3) measures of supply for services encompassing both short and long-term treatment capacity, available supply of treatment, and utilization of treatment; (4) trend measure of scheduled clinic appointments either missed or cancelled by patients and by clinics; (5) mental health provider productivity data; and (6) balancing or competing measures.

As discussed to this point, meaningful analysis and decision making requires reliable data not only on the timeliness of access but also on trends in demand for mental health services, treatments, and providers. However, understanding the availability and mix of mental health staffing, provider productivity, and treatment capacity is critical as well.

VHA Mental Health Staffing and Productivity Data

According to VHA's informal survey of frontline mental health professionals, 71 percent reported that, in their opinion, their facilities did not have adequate mental health staff to meet current demand for care. Supply of mental health staff can be reflected in terms of the number and mix of providers, as well as the productivity of available providers. Although VHA collects and reports mental health staffing and productivity data, the complexity of the computations and inaccuracies in some of the data sources presently hinders the usability of productivity information by VHA decision makers to fully assess current capacity, determine optimal resource distribution, evaluate productivity across the system, and establish mental health staffing and productivity standards.

The primary offices that generate mental health staffing information in VHA are the Allocation Resource Center (ARC) and the Office of Productivity, Efficiency, and Staffing (OPES). The ARC and OPES have different purposes for generating and disseminating this information—the ARC generates the information for budget planning and allocation purposes; OPES generates it to construct productivity models intended to assist VHA managers in making resource management decisions, primarily at the facility level.

ARC Staffing Reports

In 2005, the ARC introduced a series of Mental Health Tracking Reports to report VHA's status on the Mental Health Enhancement Initiative, a special purpose fund created to support VA's implementation of a mental health strategic plan.

ARC staffing reports show full-time employee equivalents (FTE) for "Core Mental Health Staff," which broadly includes psychiatrists; psychologists and psychology aides and technicians; social workers and social work aides and technicians; registered nurses, licensed practical nurse, licensed vocational nurses, and nurses aides; physician extenders, including nurse practitioners, physician assistants, clinical nurse specialists, and pharmacists; and therapists, including physical therapists, occupational therapists, and other types of therapists. Users can also drill down in the ARC's web-based staffing reports to determine FTE levels for specific disciplines, as well as analyze staffing at the facility, VISN, or national level. The reports do not include FTE for non-VA providers, such as contract or fee basis physicians. The primary data sources for the ARC reported FTE are DSS, VA's cost accounting system, and Financial Management System.

Table 2. ARC Selected Mental Health Staffing for 2008–2011

FTE	2008	2009	Percent Change 2008–09	2010	Percent Change 2009–10	2011	Percent Change 2010–11	Overall Change 2008–11
Mental Health Core Staffing	17,127.2	19,252.5	12.4%	20,853.9	8.3%	22,032.0	5.6%	28.6%
Physician Only	2,073.1	2,288.1	10.4%	2,452.8	7.2%	2,544.1	3.7%	22.7%
Psychologist Only	1,788.5	2,122.7	18.7%	2,464.9	16.1%	2,613.5	6.0%	46.1%
Social Worker Only	2,844.8	3,510.9	23.4%	4,155.2	18.4%	4,725.7	13.7%	66.1%

Source: Allocation Resource Center, Core Mental Health Staff by VISN accessed on February 2, 2012.

As Table 2 shows, the number of core mental health staff has increased by about 29 percent since 2008; although, the annual rate of increase each year has declined. The largest increases over the 4-year period have occurred with social worker FTE (not including social work aides or technicians) and psychologist FTE (not including psychology aides or technicians), for which FTE increased by 66 and 46 percent, respectively, between 2008 and 2011. Physician FTE increased 23 percent during the same period.

OPES Staffing and Productivity Reports

OPES' role is to develop tools that VHA managers can use to assess and optimize clinical productivity.[12] Examples of resources available from OPES include workforce reports for specialty programs, including mental health, and the Physician Productivity Cube.

OPES' Mental Health Workforce reports show staffing levels for physicians (psychiatrists) involved in direct patient care and associated mental health providers, including psychologists, social workers, clinical nurse specialists, nurse practitioners, and physician assistants. Data for the reports is extracted from VA's payroll system and, for the physicians, labor-mapping information from DSS. Labor mapping is a process by which VHA facilities allocate employees' time to various activities, including inpatient and outpatient and clinical, administrative, research, and educational activities. (VHA's labor mapping process and definitions are discussed in more detail in the next section on productivity.)

For physician FTE, OPES uses the number of *worked* hours from the Personnel and Accounting Integrated Data System and reported *direct patient care* time by provider in DSS, plus estimated FTE for contract and fee physicians. The estimated contract and fee physician FTE is calculated based on the average workload of VA paid physicians. Since social workers, clinical nurse specialists, nurse practitioners, and physician assistants are also used by other specialties, such as medicine, and because DSS labor mapping information is not available at the individual provider level, OPES uses Budget Object Codes (accounting codes used to describes types of goods or services being purchased) and mental health Clinic Stop Codes to estimate the associated provider time dedicated to mental health.

OPES' Physician Productivity Cube, is intended for facility managers to use, in conjunction with other data, to evaluate productivity at the service or department level. According to OPES officials, the cube is most useful when it is combined with other facility-level information, such as practice models or patient complexity. The cube can assist facility managers in decision making about staffing distributions, hiring and contracting, and other resource allocation decisions.

The focus of the cube is to provide information on physician productivity. It draws from multiple data sources to calculate physician productivity, and it relies on a complex set of business rules to make the calculations. The methodology involves multi-step processes to determine: (1) workforce, (2) workload, and (3) productivity.

Workforce

The physician FTE reported in the cube represents *worked, direct patient care (or clinical) FTE* of full- and part-time VA paid physicians. Productivity is not calculated for non-physician providers. Determining physician direct care FTE involves several steps.

- **Person Class.** Every physician in VA is supposed to be mapped into a specialty (such as internal medicine, psychiatry, or surgery). This is done by assigning them a "Person Class" in the Veterans Health Information Systems and Technology Architecture (VistA), VA's integrated system of patient care software applications, in order to exercise their clinical privileges and to have their workload captured in the Patient Care Encounter application.[13] Person Class, represented by numerical codes, was originally developed in the private sector to classify providers for billing purposes; it reflects aggregate groupings, provider types, and areas of specialization or focus. For example, Person Class 182906 corresponds to aggregate grouping by medical doctor, provider-type psychiatry, and specialization geriatric psychiatry.
- **Labor Mapping.** Direct care FTE is computed using facility-reported data on the allocation of physicians' time. VHA policy requires that facilities map the time all full- and part-time VA paid physicians and dentists spend in direct patient care, administration, research, and education.[14] Labor mapping is done in DSS, the designated managerial cost accounting system for VA. VHA Directive 2011-009 describes the activities included in each time category (called Account Level Budgeter Cost Centers).
    - ***Direct Patient Care*** includes time spent in preparing, providing, and following up on the clinical needs of patients. This may include reviewing patient data, consulting with colleagues about patients, contacting patients or caregivers, and supervising

residents. Direct patient care also includes attending education programs aimed at maintaining or enhancing clinical skills.

- ***Administration*** includes time spent performing managerial or administrative duties, such as preparing performance reviews, meeting reporting requirements, managing a program or service, and participating in service, facility, national or professional society committees.
- ***Research*** includes time spent performing formal, approved health care research or activities that support approved research, such as working on projects, serving on research committees, supervising research, and writing or presenting publications. Research does *not* include clinical research where workload is captured under clinical care.
- ***Education*** includes time spent preparing for and providing formal, didactic training, such as giving classroom lectures or conferences or managing residency programs and serving on medical school committees. Education does *not* include programs taken to maintain or enhance clinical skills.

Using the Person Class and DSS labor-mapping information, OPES calculates clinical time for physicians (annotated as MD FTE(C)). The difference (A) between MD FTE and MD FTE(C) represents potential physician resources currently involved in other activities such as administration, research, and education. Based on OPES' supporting data, non-clinical psychiatrist FTE associated with administration, research, and education on aggregate represents roughly 15 percent of total physician FTE, with some facilities reporting up to 32 percent.

For psychiatrists (and other non-surgical specialties), they further adjust this FTE to *exclude* time mapped to inpatient activities. According to OPES officials, they do this because of issues with the reliability and completeness in how facilities are capturing inpatient workload data for non-surgical specialties. Therefore, the Adjusted MD FTE(C) used for calculating psychiatrist FTE (and productivity) reflects *worked, outpatient, direct patient care FTE.*

Workload

Within the cube, workload is allocated to physicians using several business rules in an effort to reduce double counting or overlap. Workload is reported in terms of patient encounters and work relative value units

(WRVU).[15] Workload is only captured for work performed "within the walls" of VHA facilities—it does not include work performed by off-site, fee basis, or contract physicians.

- **Patient Encounters and RVUs.** To determine provider workload, the cube uses monthly extracts from the National Patient Care Database, which includes outpatient and inpatient CPT codes transmitted from the Patient Care Encounter package. Workload is assigned to a specialty based on the Person Class of the first attending physician associated with the encounter. If during an encounter, a patient is seen by two physicians from *different* specialties, the workload is assigned to each physician. However, if the patient is seen by two providers from the *same* specialty, the workload is assigned only to the first listed attending physician to avoid possible double counting. Using these rules, workload is aggregated for each provider, and WRVUs are calculated using values contained in Centers for Medicare and Medicaid Services Physician Fee Schedule RVU files.
- **Inpatient Workload.** At present, there are limitations in the cube for accurately reporting *inpatient* workload for non-surgical specialties, including mental health.
  Although VHA Directive 2009-002, issued in January 2009, requires mental health providers to "document and enter encounter data on all mental health professional services provided in an inpatient setting,"[16] there does not appear to be full or consistent compliance with the directive. Therefore, it is not clear how accurate or complete the inpatient workload shown in the cube is for the non-surgical specialties. Anecdotally, OPES officials know that some medical facilities are diligent about reporting inpatient workload, while others are underreporting workload or not reporting it at all.

Productivity

Despite the fairly complex business rules for calculating direct patient care FTE and workload, the productivity calculation for psychiatrists is straightforward:

$$Productivity = WRVU \div Adjusted\ MD\ FTE\ (C)$$

In this calculation, Adjusted MD FTE(C) represents the direct outpatient clinical time physicians worked in a given fiscal period. WRVU reflects workload as measured by Work RVUs. It is important to note that if a facility is diligent about capturing inpatient psychiatry workload, the WRVU will reflect both inpatient and outpatient workload, even though the FTE reflects only outpatient effort, thereby potentially overstating productivity.

Limitations with Productivity Data

While the Physician Productivity Cube may provide a ballpark measure for looking at and benchmarking service-level or facility level productivity, it has several limitations that prevent using it as a nationwide tool to gauge the true supply and availability of mental health providers in VA. These limitations are primarily due to incomplete or inaccurate information in the data sources used to calculate productivity. Specific limitations include:

- The cube is based on numerous complex business rules resulting in various adjustments to and calculations of the source data. Consequently, reconciling to source data in the cube is cumbersome.
- The cube only shows productivity for VA paid full- and part-time physicians. It does not compute productivity for other physicians, such as contract, fee basis, or without compensation physicians, who serve veterans at VHA facilities or at non-VA facilities.
- The cube currently does not show productivity for non-physicians who may play significant roles in delivery of mental health care, including psychologists, social workers, clinical nurse specialists, nurse practitioners, and physician assistants.
- In calculating psychiatrist productivity, the cube uses only outpatient FTE because of OPES' concern that facilities are not fully or accurately capturing inpatient workload. However, for those facilities that do accurately capture inpatient workload, productivity may be overstated since the denominator is just outpatient FTE, yet the numerator is both outpatient and inpatient workload.
- FTE (and consequently productivity) is calculated based on physicians' direct patient care time, excluding administration, research, and education activities. As a result, decision makers may not get a complete picture as to the impact that non-clinical activities have on meeting patient workload demands or in terms of VA's full capacity to provide services
- The cube relies heavily on labor-mapping information contained in DSS and Person Class identified in VistA, which are self-reported by

facilities. However, there is variability in how accurately, frequently, and consistently facilities are updating DSS labor mapping data, which makes it difficult to compare productivity across facilities.

- Although the cube includes a measure of facility complexity, it cannot account for local practice approaches (such as use of interdisciplinary teams), case mix, availability of support staff, or quality issues, which limits the cube's usefulness for benchmarking between medical facilities or identifying outliers.

The next section of this report describes what measures a few, large private sector health care organizations use to monitor and manage the timeliness of access to mental health services and will review what other data VHA already collects that may inform internal assessment of access to mental health care.

Measuring Access to Mental Health Care in the Private Sector

The challenge of meeting the demand for mental health services and measuring access are not unique to VHA. We interviewed the directors of behavioral health services for three private sector health care organizations based in the Pacific Northwest, California, and the Southeast. The organizations included a large, national health care system and two regionally-based systems. All three organizations have multiple mental health clinics distributed throughout their geographic service delivery area. These clinics vary widely in size, available resources, and patient demographics. Two of the organizations use electronic medical record systems for all aspects of patient care. All three have a mechanism to refer patients to providers outside their organizations to augment the capacity or range of services provided.

Despite a decrease in outpatient utilization since 2009,[17] the private sector health care organizations reported increased demand for mental health services by as much as 20 percent over the past 2 years. The directors attributed this increase to multiple factors, including declining public community mental health resources and worsening economic and financial pressures on individuals and families. Their primary strategy to address increased demand involves actively managing their clinic capacity and efficiency. For the most part, this includes reallocating resources to open new triage and evaluation slots, transitioning stable patients back to primary care, or transitioning eligible patients from individual to group encounters.

Private sector health care organizations we contacted all used performance "dashboards" (or "scorecards") that report different dimensions of access, such as timeliness, continuity of care, efficacy of treatment engagement, capacity, patient satisfaction, and quality.

Dashboards are the key decision support tools managers use to monitor and respond to the changes in demand for mental health services. The dashboards provide managers at all levels of the organization real-time data to assess supply and demand, allowing local managers to rapidly adjust and reallocate clinical resources to meet needs and upper-level managers to quickly assess the adequacy of responses and ensure that quality of care is not compromised. Different types of dashboard reports are available within the organizations, from high-level aggregated executive summaries to point-of-care tracking sheets. Wide dissemination and visibility of the dashboards is critical to ensure performance goals are communicated and met within the organizations. For example, in local clinics, dashboards are displayed in areas for all employees to see.

Dashboards display different measures designed to track various dimensions of access (that is, timeliness, continuity of care, efficacy of treatment engagement, capacity, patient satisfaction, and quality). Directors typically use multiple measures to monitor trends within each of the dimensions. Frequently measures are complementary—improved performance for one measure may be offset by performance decline of another. The most common dimensions reflected in the dashboards are discussed below.

Timeliness of Care

When measuring timeliness of mental health services, the private sector organizations consider both new patient appointments requested through self-referral or consult requests and follow-up appointments for established patients. Measuring timeliness of new patient appointments is a key focus. For new patients, the underlying assumption is that most patients want to initiate treatment as soon as possible and typically want appointments within 2 weeks.

The organizations apply similar approaches for new patient appointments—triage, then intake, followed by treatment initiation with a goal of rapid stabilization. Triage management is also consistent between the organizations. Patients requesting services, either as walk-ins or by phone, are immediately triaged. Depending on urgency, a patient will receive active treatment for emergent cases in less than 24 hours (ideally within 6 hours), urgent cases within 48–72 hours, and routine cases within 2 weeks. For consult requests or referrals by primary and specialty care providers, clinic staff contact patients within 24 business hours after the consult request to schedule appointments.

The organizations measure "time to first appointment" as the number of days between the time the patient first requests an appointment or a consult is created by a referring provider to the day of the patient's first appointment with a mental health provider for initiation of treatment with a psychiatrist, psychologist, or mental health nurse practitioner. The scheduling software electronically captures T_0 when a clerk opens the appointment schedule to create a new patient appointment. Two of the directors we interviewed stated that they expect clinics to provide 95 percent of new patient appointments within 2 weeks of a patient's first request or a consult.

Continuity of Care and Follow-Up Appointments

The private sector organizations share a uniform goal of rapid stabilization of symptoms early in the treatment course. They strive to achieve close monitoring of new patients during the initial phase of treatment to allow for symptom assessment, initialization of medications, and monitoring for medication side effects. Their dashboards include measures of continuity of care, timely follow-up appointments, and the ability clinics have to continue treatment after a new patient's initial visit.

The directors at each organization established a pre-determined average number of visits within the first 45–60 days of an initial new patient appointment. How they achieve this goal varies. Typically, a form of recurring scheduling is used to guarantee access to 4-6 appointments within a pre-determined time frame goal. Some clinics achieve this by scheduling the entire set of appointments at the time of initial presentation; others schedule the first several appointments at the conclusion of the first treatment session.

On average, behavioral health directors expect new patients to have at least four visits within the first 45–60 days of treatment. Accordingly, the organization dashboards include measures of the length of time between subsequent visits, that is the time to the second (T_2), third (T_3), and fourth (T_4) visits.

Treatment Engagement

The private sector behavioral health directors consider treatment engagement an essential element of their access performance measures. They define engagement as both the ability to provide treatment to patients who initially seek care (capture), as well as their ability to provide continued and sustained participation in treatment after the initial visit (engagement).

As a reflection of patient engagement in treatment, the dashboards report the percent of patients who continue treatment after their initial appointment.

The percent of patient engagement—that is, the percent of patients who complete a second appointment—can be expressed as:

Engagement (E2) = (N patients with T2 appointment/N patients seeking care T0) ×100

Treatment engagement measures may also indirectly reflect the quality of care delivered. The behavioral health directors expect at least 60 percent of new patients to return for a second appointment. Some also track the patient's ability to see the same provider for their follow-up care, an important factor in establishing a strong patient-provider relationship.

Capacity

Closely monitoring availability of future appointment slots is essential to be able to respond to increased demands for service. Dashboard capacity measures include time to first available appointment, third-next available appointment,[18] and the number of available new appointments per week.

This dashboard information is particularly useful to local clinic managers and providers who can then reallocate resources required to meet patient needs. Local managers review the number of open appointments available each day, the following week, and over the following month. They assess their capacity by the type of appointment—new intakes, return appointments, medication management, and individual or group therapy. Capacity for each type of provider (such as psychiatrist, psychologist, nurse practitioners or clinical specialists, and social workers) is tracked to assist in matching patients' individual needs with the clinics' available resources. Local clinics can also predict the average number of new patients expected for treatment. If their current schedule cannot accommodate their predicted demand, they initiate an informal team meeting with providers and staff and identify ways to open more appointment slots.

In tandem with capacity measures, managers closely track the ability to maximize available patient care resources at local clinics. These measures include monitoring appointment "fill rate" (the percent of available appointment times actually utilized to deliver services), as well as "no-show" (patient fails to arrive for a scheduled appointment) and "cancelation" rates.

Most of the local private sector clinics reportedly use waiting lists when there are unexpected spikes in demand. According to one director, for about 20 percent of patients, going on a wait list was preferable to the option of seeing a provider outside the organization because these patients perceived the organization's staff to be more desirable. The longest wait, on average, was 3–4 weeks from the time a patient requested services. However, all of the directors we interviewed told us their local clinics routinely review fill rates, no-show, and cancelations and manage their wait lists in an effort to quickly move patients with the longest wait times to more timely appointments (that is, within the 2-week goal).

Patient Satisfaction

Patient satisfaction is also a key element in the dashboards. All of the organizations solicit patient input through surveys and patient-initiated feedback. The directors especially rely on patient satisfaction measures for assessment of contracted care services, where access to electronic scheduling data is not available. Some include these measures as an ongoing deliverable in their contracts. Regional managers closely review discrepancies between local clinics patient satisfaction data and other dashboard performance measures. Such conflicts frequently serve as early indicators of access, engagement, or quality issues.

Application of Private Sector Measures to VHA

VHA currently reports mental health access metrics on the VHA Support Service Center (VSSC) Systems Redesign website. Some timeliness data captured by VSSC are similar to those we reviewed from the private sector. The current VHA scheduling system is able to electronically capture a "creation date" when a clerk opens the scheduler to create a new appointment. VHA reports can include a metric parallel to the private sector "time to first appointment" by measuring the time between the "creation date" and the date of the first evaluation and treatment provided by a psychiatrist, psychologist, social worker, or other mental health provider. With adaptation and testing, the first use of an International Classification of Disease (ICD-9) code for a specific mental health diagnosis (for example, PTSD) has potential for use as the trigger to start the clock for a measure to timeliness of mental health evaluation and treatment.

Similar to private sector entities, measures of time to the second, third, and fourth mental health visit could be reported. To ensure that treatment visits are captured, the measures would need to specify the type of provider (for example, psychologist or psychiatrist) or type of service (such as evaluation, treatment visit) to avoid inclusion of complementary visits (such as educational groups). An engagement measure, such as the percentage of patients seen a threshold number of times during an initial period of treatment (for example, the first 45 days), would indirectly reflect both a facility's ability to provide serial follow-up visits during early treatment and to sustain patient involvement in the initial phase of treatment.

The inability to readily track capacity imposes a major limitation on the support tools available to VISN and facility decision makers. VHA officials reported the present scheduling software is 25 years old and the software interface is not "user-friendly." Schedulers must click between several screens during the scheduling process requiring anywhere from 30 seconds to 5 minutes to schedule an appointment. VHA officials asserted that calendar-based systems used in the private sector are quicker and more user-friendly.

Additionally, VHA officials reported that ascertaining provider availability using the existing scheduling software is challenging. Each provider may have assigned several stop codes under which the provider sees patients. The stop codes are used in part to allow for reporting of utilization of specific clinics (such as PCT). For example, a psychiatrist may use DSS stop codes 509 (psychiatry-individual), 557 (psychiatry-group), and 562 (PTSD-individual) among others to capture their outpatient work on a given day. The system will treat each stop code as if each were a separate clinic with separate schedules.

While local facilities do construct ad hoc reports to identify future appointment availability (appointments available that day, the following week, and the following month), the process is labor intensive. Measures of capacity by type of appointment (new patient, medication review, follow-up), or by type of provider (psychiatrist, psychologist, social worker, nurse practitioner) are not readily available.

Conclusion

The data and measures needed by decision makers for planning and service provision may differ at the national, VISN, and facility level. No measure of access is perfect or paints a complete picture in isolation. Meaningful analysis and decision making requires reliable data, on not only the timeliness of access but also on trends in demand for mental health services, treatments, and providers; the availability and mix of mental health staffing; provider productivity; and treatment capacity. These demand and supply variables in turn feed back upon a system's ability to provide treatment that is patient centered and timely.

Our review found that VHA's 14-day follow-up measure provides decision makers with a limited picture of a new patient's ability to access and begin mental health treatment. Additionally, depending on a veteran's point of access, this metric does not truly measure VHA's stated objective "to ensure timely access for all veterans who are new to mental health." A series of timeliness and treatment engagement measures might provide decision makers with a more comprehensive view of the ability with which new patients can access mental health treatment.

Furthermore, although VHA collects and reports mental health staffing and productivity data, the complexity of the computations and inaccuracies in some of the data sources limits the usability of productivity information to fully assess current capacity, determine optimal resource distribution, evaluate productivity across the system, and establish mental health staffing and productivity standards.

Private sector entities with whom we spoke reported that their managers use multiple measures to assess a range of access parameters. These entities disseminate their dashboard reports to all levels of management thereby facilitating timely response to changing access dynamics.

Beyond measures of timeliness (or delay) to mental health care, a dashboard of user friendly measures that incorporate aspects of patient demand, provider supply, clinic capacity, and provider productivity, anchored by a consistent set of business rules, might provide VHA decision makers with a more robust perspective from which to assess and timely respond to changes in access parameters.

Recommendations

4. We recommend the Under Secretary for Health ensure that data collection efforts related to mental health access are aligned with the operational needs of relevant decision makers throughout the organization.

Under Secretary for Health Comments

The Under Secretary for Health concurred with the OIG's findings and recommendation. VHA's Office of Mental Health Operations has developed a comprehensive mental health information system. This operations group will review available data and add other data elements as necessary, ensuring the information system is aligned to the operational needs of the organizational structure. We consider the planned actions acceptable and will follow up on the implementation.

APPENDIX A: SCOPE AND METHODOLOGY

We conducted this review from December 2011 to March 2012. To address our review objective, we reviewed applicable laws, regulations, policies, procedures, guidelines, and studies. Additionally, we focused on measures contained with the FY 2011 PAR:

- Percent of eligible patient evaluations documented within 14 days of the new mental health patient index encounter.
- Percent of specialty care appointments completed within 14 days of the desired date.

To evaluate whether patients received full evaluations within 14 days, we obtained the VSSC data "Percent of Eligible Patient Evaluations Documented within 14 days of New Mental Health Patient Index Encounter (Formerly Mental Health 14-Day Follow-up Monitor)" report for FY 2011. VHA officials identified this as the source data used to support the 95 percent reported in VA's FY 2011 PAR. We then obtained a statistically random sample to test the data. For further details on the sampling methodology, see Appendix B.

To evaluate whether patients received their mental health appointments within 14 days of the desired date, we obtained the VSSC Report "Wait Time Final Cube (Completed Appointments)" from VHA Systems Redesign. We received all new and established patient mental health appointments, excluding Compensation and Pension visits. We then obtained a statistically random sample of new patient appointments and established patient appointments to test the data. For further details on the sampling methodology, please refer to Appendix B.

We interviewed the directors of behavioral health services for three private sector health care organizations based in the Pacific Northwest, California, and the Southeast. The organizations included a large, national health care system and two regionally based systems. All three organizations have multiple mental health clinics distributed throughout their geographic service delivery area. These clinics vary widely in size, available resources, and patient demographics. Two of the organizations use electronic medical record systems for all aspects of patient care. All three have a mechanism to refer patients to providers outside their organizations to augment the capacity or range of services provided. During the review, we visited four VA medical centers located in:

- Denver, CO
- Milwaukee, WI
- Salisbury, NC
- Spokane, WA

While on site at VA healthcare facilities, we conducted interviews with schedulers, providers and medical center management to identify the steps used to schedule appointments, the origins of return to clinic dates used by providers, and the clinic availability of the providers. The audit team used these interviews to determine if VHA personnel followed established scheduling procedures.

We assessed the reliability of automated data by comparing three selected data elements—create date of appointment, desired date of care, date of completed appointment—to the electronic medical records. To test completeness of the data, we captured and compared all completed appointments from Spokane found in VistA and confirmed the completed appointments were included in VHA's universes used to calculate and support the performance measures. We concluded that the data used to accomplish the audit objective was sufficiently reliable.

Our assessment of internal controls focused only on those controls related to the accuracy of veterans' waiting times and access to care. The Office of Audits and Evaluations and Office of Healthcare Inspections completed this review jointly in accordance with The Council of the Inspectors General on Integrity and Efficiency's Quality Standards for Inspection and Evaluation.

Appendix B: Statistical Sampling Methodology

To determine whether veterans can access the mental health care that they need in a timely manner, we reviewed three random samples to ensure veterans seeking VHA mental health services for the first time received timely evaluations, and to ensure accurate recording of waiting times for new and established mental health patients.

- Eligible Patient Evaluations – New Mental Health Patient Index Encounter
- Completed mental health appointments for new patients
- Completed mental health appointments for established patients

Population

The population of encounters (appointments) of veterans seeking mental health care at VHA for the first time (Sample 1) consisted of over 373,000 in FY 2011. These veterans have had no prior encounters in specific mental health clinics in the previous 24 months at that specific medical center, and require further evaluation and treatment in mental health. In the FY 2011 PAR, VHA reported 95 percent of these veterans received an extensive evaluation and initiation of appropriate mental health care within 14 days of a trigger encounter.

The population of appointments for veterans new to a specific mental health clinic (Sample 2) consisted of over 262,000 completed appointments in FY 2011. The definition of a new patient is someone not seen by a high-level qualified provider within the prior 24 month. A patient will only move into the "established" category once a high-level, qualified physician has seen them. The population of appointments for veterans established in the mental health clinic (Sample 3) consisted of over 10 million completed appointments in FY 2011.

In the FY 2011 PAR, VHA reported they completed 95 percent of new and established specialty care appointments within 14 days of the desired date. We obtained and reviewed only the mental health patient (all 500 series stop codes) appointments and separated them into universes of new and established patient appointments. VHA's mental health appointment data showed 95 percent of the new patient and 98 percent of the established patient appointments were completed within 14 days of the desired date.

Sampling Design

We used a simple random sampling approach to select the sample from each of the three populations, based on a design precision of no more than 8.2 percent of the estimated number of cases, a 90 percent confidence level, and an expected error rate of no more than 10 percent of the total. This sampling technique provided equal chance of selection of all records in the respective population. Based on this sampling criterion, we used a classical simple random formula to calculate the sample sizes.

We segregated the populations of records into two groups based on two judgmentally selected sites and all remaining sites. Each randomly selected sample was within the two groups. OIG statisticians used a random number generator to generate a random selection of appointments, which automatically selected records from the population.

Table 3. Sampling Approach New Mental Health Evaluations

Group	Total No. Of Sites	Total Evaluations	Sample Size
Certainty Sites	2	5,700	53
Remaining Sites	139	367,600	93
Total	141	373,300	146

Source: VA OIG.

Table 4. Sampling Approach New Patient Completed Appointments

Group	Total No. Of Sites	Total Appointments	Sample Size
Certainty Sites	2	4,300	60
Remaining Sites	139	257,900	200
Total	141	262,200	260

Source: VA OIG.

Table 5. Sampling Approach Established Patient Completed Appointments

Group	Total No. Of Sites	Total Appointments	Sample Size
Certainty Sites	2	135,800	60
Remaining Sites	139	9,908,700	200
Total	141	10,045,500	260

Source: VA OIG.

Sampling Methodology

The 146 sampled evaluations in Sample 1, and the 260 sampled appointments each in Samples 2 and 3 represented particular segments of the overall universes. We accounted for differences in the probability of selection between groups by weighting the sample results.

To evaluate access to mental health care and determine if veterans received a full evaluation within 14 days, we identified when the patient initially contacted mental health seeking services, or when another provider referred the patient to mental health. Specifically, we used VA's

Compensation and Pension Records Interchange to review patients' visit dates, clinical notes, and consult records. We determined if the full evaluation contained patient history, diagnosis, and treatment plan. Based on that information, we calculated the number of days between initial contact in mental health and the full mental health evaluation.

To evaluate wait times for mental health appointments, we determined if VHA personnel followed established procedures when selecting the types of appointments and veterans' desired dates of care. Specifically, we reviewed the desired date of care requested by the provider and documented in medical records or the veteran's desired date of care as recorded in the VistA scheduling and consult packages by the scheduler. Based on that information, we calculated the number of days between the desired date and the completed appointment date.

Estimates and Margins of Error

Based on the results of our three samples, we projected nationwide totals and percentages of delays to evaluations, and waiting times for new and established mental health appointments. We used WesVar software to calculate the weighted population estimates and associated sampling errors. WesVar employs replication methodology to calculate margins of error and confidence intervals that correctly account for the complexity of the sample design. The margins of error and confidence intervals are indicators of the precision of estimates. If we repeated this audit with multiple samples, the confidence intervals would differ for each sample, but would include the true population value 90 percent of the time. The projected numbers are rounded to agree with the numbers in the report.

Sample 1

We projected that only 184,000 (49 percent) of over 373,000 new mental health patient evaluations were completed within VHA's goal of 14 days. Table 6 shows the results of our sample.

Sample 2

We projected that approximately 168,000 (64 percent) of new patient appointments were completed within 14 days of the desired date. Table 7 shows the results of our sample.

Table 6. Projections New Mental Health Patient Evaluations

Attribute	Projected Evaluations	Projected Percent	Margin of Error Based on 90 Percent Confidence Interval			Sample Size
			Margin of Error	Lower Limit	Upper Limit	
Evaluation Within 14 Days	184,000	49.4	32,764	151,643	217,171	67
Evaluation Later Than 14 Days	161,000	43.1	32,206	128,784	193,195	68
Evaluation Not Completed	28,000	7.5	16,770	11,123	44,662	11
Total	373,000	100	16,775	356,513	390,064	146

Source: VA OIG.

Table 7. Projections New Patient Completed Appointments

Attribute	Projected Appointments	Projected Percent	Margin of Error Based on 90 Percent Confidence Interval			Sample Size
			Margin of Error	Lower Limit	Upper Limit	
Wait Time Within 14 Days	168,000	64.1	14,497	153,509	182,503	175
Wait Time Over 14 Days	94,000	35.9	14,497	79,734	108,728	85
Total	262,000	100.0				260

Source: VA OIG

Sample 3

We projected that approximately 8.8 million (88 percent) of follow-up appointments within 14 days of the desired date. Table 8 shows the results of our sample.

Table 8. Projections Established Patient Completed Appointments

Attribute	Projected Appointments	Projected Percent	Margin of Error Based on 90 Percent Confidence Interval			Sample Size
			Margin of Error	Lower Limit	Upper Limit	
Wait Time Within 14 Days	8,838,900	88.0	376,936	8,460,951	9,214,822	227
Wait Time Over 14 Days	1,207,000	12.0	376,936	829,665	1,583,536	33
Total	10,045,000	100.0				260

Source: VA OIG.

APPENDIX C: PREVIOUS OIG REPORTS HIGHLIGHTING NEED FOR IMPROVED APPOINTMENT SCHEDULING AND PERFORMANCE MEASURES

Audit of VHA's Outpatient Scheduling Procedures, Report No. 04-02887-169, July 8, 2005

Schedulers did not follow established procedures when selecting the type of appointment when entering the desired appointment date, which affected how the waiting time was calculated. The then Under Secretary for Health agreed to ensure medical facility managers require schedulers to create appointments following established procedures and monitor the schedulers' use of correct procedures when creating appointments.

Audit of VHA's Outpatient Waiting Times, Report No. 07-00616-199, September 10, 2007

Schedulers were not following established procedures for making and recording medical appointments, and schedulers were not receiving annual training. The then Under Secretary for Health agreed to establish procedures to routinely test the accuracy of reported waiting times and completeness of electronic waiting lists and take corrective action when testing shows questionable differences between the desired dates of care shown in medical records and documented in the VistA scheduling package. The Under Secretary also agreed to ensure schedulers received required annual training.

Audit of Alleged Manipulation of Waiting Times in VISN 3, Report No. 07-03505-129, May 19, 2008

The U.S. Senate Committee on Veterans' Affairs requested we review allegations that leadership at VISN 3 was manipulating procedures to misrepresent patient waiting times. Schedulers were not following appointment scheduling procedures or inputting the correct desired appointment date. The then Under Secretary for Health did not agree with the recommendations to monitor compliance with established policies since the issues cited for VISN 3 reflected the need for national solutions that VHA was already addressing in response to previous reports.

Healthcare Inspection of Access to VA Mental Health Care for Montana Veterans, Report No. 08-00069-102, March 31, 2009

VHA needed to increase the availability of evidence-based psychotherapy for mental health services in rural Montana. The then Under Secretary for Health agreed with the findings and took action to expand evidence-based psychotherapy with additional resources and developing contracts with providers throughout the state.

Healthcare Inspection of Electronic Waiting List Management for Mental Health Clinics Atlanta VA Medical Center, Report No. 10-02986-215, July 12, 2011

The inspection suggested that VHA improve performance measures for mental health care waiting times because medical centers may be compliant with current performance measures but may not be providing timely treatment.

Review of Select Patient Care Delays and Reusable Medical Equipment Review, Central Texas Veterans Health Care System, Report No. 11-03941-61, January 6, 2012

Appointments were routinely made incorrectly by using the next available appointment date instead of the patient's desired date. The Director agreed to ensure staff follow VA policy for scheduling outpatient appointments and monitor compliance.

APPENDIX D: DETAILED LEGEND FOR FIGURES

For the figures in this report:

- The color green is used to illustrate primary care venues and the flow of patients seeking care at VA facilities who have not received a completed comprehensive diagnostic and treatment planning evaluation by a specialized mental health (MH) provider. 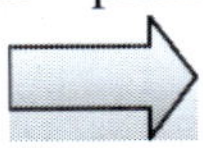
- The color blue is used to denote specialized MH venues  and the flow of patients once they have received a completed comprehensive diagnostic and treatment planning evaluation. 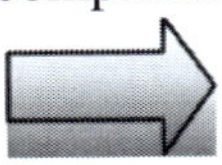
- Light purple is used to denote care at VA readjustment counseling centers (Vet Centers). 
- Light red is used to denote care at non-VHA settings including private MH providers, community MH services, and MH services accessed via other agencies (e.g. Tricare-DOD, Indian Health Service) or fee basis care arranged through VHA. 
- Orange is used to denote VHA inpatient/residential treatment venues. 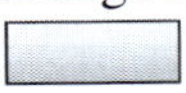
- A small square containing the number 1 is used to denote VHA access measure 1 (percent of eligible patient evaluations documented within 14 days of new MH patient index encounter). Placement of the small square completely within the lower corner of a MH treatment venue

box is used to indicate that the MH index encounter and completed comprehensive evaluation have occurred within the same day at the same MH venue. The color inside the small square therefore shifts from green (non-MH) to blue (specialty MH) to indicate that the measure 1 clock essentially starts at point in time 1 and end at point in time 1. The arrow that precedes the small square is green while the arrow following the small square to reflect the transition to specialty MH treatment.

Placement of a small, completely blue square partly above and partly within an upper corner of a MH venue box is used to denote VHA access measure 1 when the initial MH trigger encounter precedes the encounter within which a comprehensive diagnostic evaluation is completed. The completed evaluation may occur within the same specialty MH venue as the trigger MH encounter, for example, general MH clinic (MHC) at point in time 1 and MHC at point in time 2 or within different MH venues, for example, MH walk-in clinic at point in time 1 and a Women's Stress Disorders Treatment Team (WSDTT) clinic at point in time 2. The arrow between the trigger encounter MH venue and the MH venue at which the comprehensive evaluation is completed is shaded from green to blue to indicate capture by the measure of the time frame between encounters at each venue and the transition to specialty MH care. The arrow subsequently following the MH venue box would then be shaded completely blue. 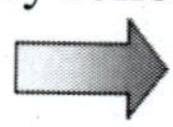

- A small, blue square containing the number 2 is used to denote VHA access measure 2, MH follow-up within 7 days of discharge from an inpatient or residential treatment unit. The measure captures the time between the point at which a discharge is entered into the system, and the point in time at which the follow-up MH encounter occurs. 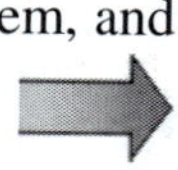
- A small, blue and yellow square containing the number 3 is used to denote VHA access measure 3, OEF/OIF veterans new to MH receiving 8 weeks of psychotherapy within 14 weeks. 

- Blue ovals are used in figure 2 to represent specific types of MH treatment services; medication management (Med Mgmt, Evidence based psychotherapy (EBT), other psychotherapies (Other Therapy), case management (Case Mgmt), counseling, and education groups.

APPENDIX E: UNDER SECRETARY FOR HEALTH COMMENTS

Department of Veterans Affairs
Memorandum
Date: April 12, 2012
From: Under Secretary for Health (10)
Subj: OIG Draft Report, Veterans Health Administration: Review of Veterans' Access to Mental Health Care
To: Assistant Inspector General for Audits and Evaluations (52)

1) The Veterans Health Administration (VHA) is unequivocally committed to providing the best care possible for Veterans and will act rapidly on all findings that may improve Veterans' access to mental health care. I have reviewed the draft report and generally agree with the report recommendations. VHA leadership and staff will continue to review the data, findings, and conclusions drawn in this draft report carefully to identify how best to meet Veterans' needs.
2) VHA is currently reviewing several issues that affect the ability to evaluate patient wait time performance measurement. These issues include provider and team behavior, scheduler system practices, as well as methodology.
3) The Office of Inspector General (OIG) assessed documentation at four VHA facilities. VHA will conduct a more extensive review of all VISNs using the approach developed by OIG. Based on the time needed to do these reviews and the value of the information obtained, VHA may expand the analysis to additional facilities in at least some VISNs. The goal is to develop a comprehensive set of information about how policies and practices work and what needs to be done to accurately assess wait times.
4) Attachment A provides our observations about the metrics that OIG reviewed.
5) Thank you for the opportunity to review the draft report. A complete action plan is attached. If you have any questions, please contact Linda H. Lutes, Director, Management Review Service (10A4A4) at (202) 4617014.

(original signed by:)
Robert A. Petzel, M.D.

Attachments

ATTACHMENT A: DESCRIPTION OF MEASURES

A. Metric: First-Time Patient's Access to a Full Mental Health Evaluation

1) The first metric, labeled in the report as "First-Time Patient's Access to a Full Mental Health Evaluation," was developed in 2007. It assesses the time that it takes for a Veteran to receive a full mental health evaluation and treatment initiation if they have never previously had such a mental health service at VA. VHA mandated this be completed within 14 days after an initial 24-hour period in which a triage evaluation was completed (i.e., a total of 15 days from initial referral). This distinction is important because in the first 24 hours after the determination that a Veteran without mental health treatment in the last 24 months needs mental health care, a triage evaluation is required, but this often is done without a specific appointment; the mental health provider typically sees the Veteran in Primary Care, the Emergency Department, at a walk-in clinic, or in some other way for this triage evaluation within 24 hours. After triage, the patient may be immediately admitted to an inpatient service if the need is urgent. If not, the appointment must be made at that time and occur with the next 14 days.
2) The OIG reports (page i) that this measure "is not a meaningful measure of waiting time." We agree with this finding. This was never intended to measure wait time, but rather, as the OIG suggests, it was intended to "measure how long it took VHA to conduct the evaluation."

B. Metric: New Patient Waiting Time

1) The second metric, "New Patient Waiting Time" as measured per the scheduling directive, refers to appointments for patients who are new to a specific mental health clinic. That is, they may already have contact in one or more other mental health clinics, so they are not *new* to VA mental health care in general. The VHA scheduling directive

requires schedulers to ask Veterans when they want to be seen for a new appointment. This is the *Desired Date*. The report indicates that OIG did not use that prescribed VHA methodology to assess the accuracy of this waiting time metric. Rather, OIG assessed waiting time based on the time that the appointment was actually entered into the system - the *Create Date*.

2) We agree with OIG's concerns that use of the *Desired Date* leads to ambiguity of the interaction between the patient and the scheduler. A simplified methodology would significantly improve the reliability of the new patient scheduling data. This is one of the issues that VHA is currently reviewing.

C. Metric: Follow-up Appointments

The third metric, "Follow-up Appointments" uses a similar method as described for the second metric "New Patient Waiting Time." We generally agree that some revision of the metric is required. This is one of the issues that VHA is currently reviewing.

VETERANS HEALTH ADMINISTRATION

Action Plan

OIG Draft Report, Veterans Health Administration: Review of Veterans' Access to Mental Health Care

Date of Draft Report: March 23, 2012

Recommendations/Actions	Status	Completion Date

Recommendation 1: We recommended that the Under Secretary for Health revise the current full mental health evaluation measurement to ensure the measurement is calculated to reflect the veteran's wait time experience upon contact with the mental health clinic or the veteran's referral to the mental health service from another provider to the completion of the evaluation.

VHA Comment

Concur

The Veterans Health Administration (VHA) concurs with the Office of Inspector General (OIG) about the importance of ensuring that VHA's measurement of waiting times is meaningful and reflective of the Veteran's wait time experience. VHA leadership has consistently emphasized the critical importance of ensuring Veterans have timely access to mental health care with Veteran Integrated Service Networks (VISN) and facilities. While VHA changed its definition of access and designated measures in Fiscal Year (FY) 2012 to capture information about timely follow up care for specific high risk populations, these new measures do not directly address the "wait time experience" for all Veterans seeking mental health services.

VHA has convened a work group to specifically examine how best to measure Veterans' wait time experiences. This work group will develop an action plan to create new metrics about how long it takes to get care (such as wait time from referral to evaluation, or timeliness of treatment initiation) for Veterans using mental health treatment. The action plan will be provided to the Under Secretary for Health (USH) for review on or before July 1, 2012.

In process Work group plan will be provided to the Under Secretary for Health (USH) for review NLT July 1, 2012.

Recommendation 2: We recommended that the Under Secretary for Health reevaluate alternative measures or combinations of measures that could effectively and accurately reflect the patient experience of access to mental health appointments.

VHA Comment

Concur

VHA is committed to developing a combination of measures that will reliably and accurately capture appointment scheduling performance for new and ongoing treatment.

Appointment scheduling measures should be sufficiently flexible to accommodate a Veteran's condition and the phase of treatment. For example, for Veterans who need weekly evidence-based psychotherapy training, a 14-day policy for time between appointments could be too long. At the other end of the spectrum, for a Veteran on a maintenance schedule after successful treatment, a return appointment in 14 days would be much too soon. Instead, a thoughtful, individualized maintenance plan should be developed to guide the timing of return appointments. The work group described in the response to Recommendation 1 will develop a set of options for measuring scheduling processes based upon Veterans' treatment needs considering the complexity and severity of problems identified and the phase of treatment.

In Process Work group plan to be provided to USH for review NLT July 1, 2012

Recommendation 3: We recommended that the Under Secretary for Health conduct a staffing analysis to determine if mental health staff vacancies represent a systemic issue impeding the Veterans Health Administration's ability to meet mental health timeliness goals, and if so, develop an action plan to correct the impediments.

VHA Comment

Concur

VHA facility mental health staffing has historically been determined at the facility level to allow flexibility to staff based upon provider pools, types of programs offered, and Veteran demand.

VHA has recently developed a prototype staffing model for general mental health outpatient care using the same methodology as was used to successfully develop its Primary Care staffing model. The methodology included a literature review, interviews with other healthcare systems, and use of available productivity data. The prototype mental health staffing model is currently being piloted within three Veterans Integrated Service Networks (VISN) to validate its effectiveness prior to field implementation. National implementation of the model is targeted for September 30, 2012.

VHA began collecting monthly vacancy data about mental health direct care positions as of January 31, 2012. A survey collects information by facility and discipline on the number of authorized positions for mental health and the number of vacant positions so that vacancy rates can be accurately calculated. VHA is currently assessing the impact of vacancies on operations and developing recommendations for improvement.

In Process National mental health staffing guidance to be implemented NLT September, 30, 2012.

VHA evaluation of vacancy data and related recommendations to be provided to USH NLT July 31, 2012

Recommendation 4: We recommended that the Under Secretary for Health ensure that data collection efforts related to mental health access are aligned with the operational needs of relevant decision makers throughout the organization.

VHA Comment

Concur

In March 2011, VHA established an Office of Mental Health Operations with operational oversight of the VHA Mental Health Program. Each VISN has identified a Mental Health Lead to collaborate with VHA Central Office and facility mental health providers. This VHA mental health organizational structure facilitates information sharing and best practices.

In FY 2011, VHA developed a comprehensive mental health information system. This system is available to all VHA staff to support management decisions and quality improvement efforts. Current VHA performance metrics and quantitative data are made available. The system provides normative information on utilization and penetration of VHA mental health services by facilities within each VISN, or nationally within treatment domains (e.g., substance abuse services, post-traumatic stress disorder, and general mental health). VHA will review existing available data and add other data elements related to access as developed by the work group referenced in the response to Recommendation 1 to ensure that the mental health information system is aligned to the operational needs of the established VHA mental health organizational structure.

In Process Data elements related to mental health access identified by the work groups referenced in the response to Recommendation 1 will be added to the mental health information system NLT September 30, 2012

Veterans Health Administration
April 2012

End Notes

[1] Millman, M., Access to Healthcare in America, Institute of Medicine, Washington D.C., The National Academies Press, 1993.

[2] Managing Managed Care: Quality Improvement in Behavioral Health, Institute of Medicine, Washington D.C., The National Academies Press, 1997.

[3] A stop code is a three-digit outpatient workload identifier that indicates the main clinical group responsible for care. Outpatient mental health clinics are indicated by stop codes 500–599. For patient encounters, primary and secondary stop codes can be indicated.

[4] A Person Class is a six-digit identifier used to classify providers by discipline, specialty, and subspecialty.

[5] Gerard Gallucci, M.D., M.H.S.; Wayne Swartz, L.C.S.W.-C.; Florence Hackerman, L.C.P.C., *Brief Reports: Impact of the Wait for an Initial Appointment on the Rate of Kept Appointments at a Mental Health Center*, Psychiatric Services, Vol. 56 No.3, March 1, 2005.

[6] Hoffman, K.A., et al., *Days to treatment and early retention among patients in treatment for alcohol drug disorders,* Addictive Behaviors (2011), doi:10.1016/j.addbeh.2011.01.031.

[7] VHA Handbook 1160.01, *Uniform Mental Health Services in VA Medical Centers and Clinics*, September 11, 2008.

[8] "Mental Health 14-Day Follow-Up Monitor Documentation," Last Updated 4/20/2011. Accessed at VHA Support Service Center (VSSC) website.

[9] Hunt I.M., Kapur N., Webb R., Robinson J., Burns J., Shaw J., and Appleby L., *Suicide in recently discharged psychiatric patients: a case-control study*, Psychological Medicine, 2009, 39, 443-449.

[10] *Suicide After Psychiatric Hospitalization*. Review of Hunt I.M. et al. (cited in previous footnote), Journal Watch Psychiatry, May 11, 2009.

[11] Qin, Ping and Nordentoft, Merete, *Suicide Risk in Relation to Psychiatric Hospitalization*, Archives of General Psychiatry, Volume 62, April 2005, p.427-432.

[12] VHA Support Service Center (VSSC) website, OPES Mission, http://opes.vssc.med.va.gov/Pages/Default.aspx, accessed on 1/30/12.

[13] VHA Directive 2005-059, *Person Class File Taxonomy*, December 7, 2005.

[14] VHA Directive 2011-009, *Physician and Dentist Labor Mapping*, February 28, 2011.

[15] RVUs are widely used in the health care industry to reflect the resources required to perform medical procedures (designated by Current Procedural Terminology or CPT codes) and are used as the basis for reimbursement under Medicare and other health insurance. Procedures comprise three RVUs—Work RVUs reflect the time and intensity to perform a procedure in relation to other procedures, Malpractice RVUs reflect the costs related to maintaining malpractice insurance, and Practice RVUs reflect the costs associated with maintaining a medical practice. For workload measurement and productivity, only the WRVUs are relevant.

[16] VHA Directive 2009-002, *Patient Care Data Capture*, January 23, 2009.

[17] Johnson, Avery, Jonathan D. Rockoff, and Anna Wilde Mathews. "Americans Cut Back on Visits to Doctors," *The Wall Street Journal,* July 29, 2010.

[18] The third-next available appointment open for scheduling eliminates overestimates of available services caused by high no-show or cancelation rates, which reduce the "1st next available" wait time.

In: Veterans' Access to Mental Health Care
Editor: Edgar W. Schneider
ISBN: 978-1-63485-195-4

Chapter 5

Veterans Health Administration: Audit of VHA's Efforts to Improve Veterans' Access to Outpatient Psychiatrists*

VA Office of Inspector General

Acronyms

CPT	Current Procedure Terminology
FY	Fiscal Year
FTE	Full-Time Equivalent
OIG	Office of Inspector General
OMHO	Office of Mental Health Operations
OPES	Office of Productivity, Efficiency, and Staffing
RVU	Relative Value Unit
VA	Department of Veterans Affairs
VAMC	Veterans Affairs Medical Center
VHA	Veterans Health Administration
VISN	Veterans Integrated Service Network

* This is an edited, reformatted and augmented version of Report No. 13-03917-487, issued by the Department of Veterans Affairs, Office of Inspector General, August 25, 2015.

REPORT HIGHLIGHTS: AUDIT OF VHA'S EFFORTS TO IMPROVE VETERANS' ACCESS TO OUTPATIENT PSYCHIATRISTS

Why We Did This Audit

We evaluated the Veterans Health Administration's (VHA) efforts to improve veterans' access to outpatient psychiatrists. The Office of Inspector General's (OIG) 2012 *Review of Veterans' Access to Mental Health Care* identified a bottleneck in access to psychiatrists.

What We Found

VHA has not been fully effective in its use of hiring opportunities or its use of existing personnel to improve veterans' access to psychiatrists. From fiscal year (FY) 2012 through FY 2014, VHA increased outpatient psychiatrist full-time equivalents (FTEs) by almost 15 percent. During that time, the number of veterans' outpatient encounters with psychiatrists increased by about 10 percent, and the number of individual veterans who received outpatient care from a psychiatrist increased about 9 percent.

We found that VHA did not have an effective method for establishing psychiatrist staffing needs. Throughout recent hiring initiatives, VHA did not stress a specific need for psychiatrists; instead, facilities determined their own staffing needs. VHA did not ensure facilities used consistent and effective clinic management practices.

This resulted in 94 of 140 health care facilities that needed additional psychiatrist FTEs to meet demand, as of December 2014. We found VHA facilities could have better used about 25 percent of psychiatrist FTE clinical time to see veterans in FY 2014, which equated to nearly $113.5 million in psychiatrists' pay. Over the next 5 years, this would equate to over $567 million if clinic management is not strengthened now.

What We Recommended

We recommended the Under Secretary for Health ensure facilities incorporate the Office of Mental Health Operations staffing model to determine the appropriate number of psychiatrists needed, and attain appropriate staffing levels or identify alternative options. We recommended the Under Secretary develop clinic management business rules, reassess the appropriateness of VHA's productivity target for psychiatrists, and develop a mechanism to monitor the variance in which psychiatrists code encounters.

Agency Comments

The Under Secretary for Health concurred with our findings and recommendations and provided an appropriate action plan. We will follow up on the implementation of the corrective actions.

LINDA A. HALLIDAY
Deputy Inspector General

INTRODUCTION

Objective

Our objective was to evaluate the Veterans Health Administration's (VHA) efforts to improve veterans' access to outpatient psychiatrists.

Prior Reports

The Office of Inspector General's (OIG) 2012 *Review of Veterans' Access to Mental Health Care* (Report No. 12-00900-168, April 23, 2012), identified a bottleneck in psychiatrists' appointments and reported that, at the four facilities visited, psychiatrists generally were not available for the next 41 days, on average. In addition, three of the four facilities had vacant psychiatrist positions.

OIG's 2012 *Audit of VHA's Physician Staffing Levels for Specialty Care Services* (Report No. 11-01827-35, December 27, 2012), identified that VHA did not establish productivity standards for 31 of 33 specialty care services, including psychiatrists, and VA medical facility management did not develop staffing plans. VHA responded to OIG recommendations by establishing productivity standards for psychiatrists and other specialty care services.

Program Size

In fiscal year (FY) 2014, VHA spent nearly $6.7 billion on mental health care services. Of that, nearly $4 billion was used for VA outpatient mental health care, which included outpatient psychiatry services. The $4 billion was over 24 percent more than VHA spent for outpatient mental health care in FY 2012. During FY 2014, VHA employed an average of about 2,800 psychiatrist full-time equivalents (FTEs) and paid them over $733 million in salaries and benefits. Of those psychiatrists, VHA allocated nearly 1,800 psychiatrist FTEs to provide outpatient clinical care during FY 2014. Clinical outpatient FTE time excludes non-working time such as annual and sick leave. Those VHA psychiatrists treated nearly 870,000 individual veterans during FY 2014.

Importance of Psychiatrists to Mental Health

Psychiatrists are more expensive than other mental health clinicians, and often difficult to recruit. In a May 2012 internal memo, VHA stated workload concerns about the average number of veterans treated by a psychiatrist in a year and the average number of visits veterans receive per year. Specifically, VHA stated a significant proportion of VA psychiatrists saw in excess of 800 to 900 veterans per year and some veterans were only seen once per year due to access demands.

VHA Hiring Initiatives

On April 19, 2012, the former Secretary of Veterans Affairs announced VHA would hire approximately 1,600 additional mental health clinicians. On May 8, 2012, the former Secretary of Veterans Affairs testified to Congress that psychiatrists are the toughest to recruit, and that of the 1,600 additional clinicians, VHA planned to hire about 57 psychiatrists. On June 3, 2013, VHA announced it successfully hired over 1,600 new mental health clinicians and filled over 2,000 existing mental health clinician vacancies. In August 2014, VA initiated plans to hire over 2,700 additional mental health clinicians as part of a VHA-wide hiring effort in response to Public Law 113-146, the Veterans Access, Choice, and Accountability Act of 2014.

Nationwide Pay Exception for Psychiatrists

In May 2012, the then-Under Secretary for Health approved a nationwide blanket pay exception for psychiatrists. The pay exception expanded the pay range maximum amount from $195,000 to $250,000. According to VHA, the pay exception allowed facility directors the ability to offer a more competitive salary to a recruited psychiatrist without an individual exception request to VHA, saving valuable time.

Effective November 30, 2014, VHA moved psychiatrists from Pay Table 1 to Pay Table 2, and increased the maximum annual pay amount for Pay Table 2, Tier 1 to $240,000 ($250,000 for Tier 2). As a result, VHA officials stated the nationwide pay exception for psychiatrists was no longer necessary and VHA rescinded the exception effective November 30, 2014.

Office of Mental Health Operations Staffing Model

During 2014, VHA's Office of Mental Health Operations (OMHO) developed a ratio to determine a minimum psychiatrist staffing level for facilities. OMHO determined the minimum ratio to be 1.22 outpatient psychiatrist FTEs per 1,000 individual mental health patients. OMHO derived the 1.22 ratio based on the median level of psychiatrists at VA medical facilities nationwide. OMHO stated the model was used as guidance for hiring psychiatrists at facilities in which psychiatrists were underrepresented in mental health clinics.

Other Information

- Appendix A provides details on our scope and methodology.
- Appendix B provides potential monetary benefits.

RESULTS AND RECOMMENDATIONS

Finding: VHA Needs to Further Improve Veterans' Access to Psychiatrists

VITA has not been fully effective in its use of hiring opportunities or its use of existing personnel to improve veterans' access to psychiatrists. During FY 2014, VITA spent nearly $4 billion in outpatient mental health care services—over 24 percent more funding than in FY 2012—and increased outpatient psychiatrist FTEs by almost 15 percent. During that time, from FY 2012 through FY 2014, veterans' encounters with outpatient psychiatrists increased by about 10 percent, and individual veterans who received outpatient care from a psychiatrist increased by about 9 percent. An encounter represents an appointment between a patient and a clinician responsible for diagnosing, evaluating, and treating the patient's condition. Some veterans have multiple encounters with an outpatient psychiatrist per year.

VITA did not have an effective method for establishing psychiatrist staffing needs at VA medical facilities. During a 2012 hiring initiative and throughout recent hiring efforts, VITA did not stress a specific need for psychiatrists; instead, it provided Veteran Integrated Service Networks (VISNs) and facilities the latitude to determine their own staffing needs using their own methods. In addition, VITA did not ensure facilities used consistent and effective clinic management practices, resulting in inefficiencies and a high rate of clinical time that was not used for patient care during FY 2014.

VITA's focus on meeting its hiring goals instead of focusing on hiring the appropriate number of mental health clinicians at the appropriate specific facility contributed to 94 of 140 facilities needing additional psychiatrist FTEs to meet veteran demand, as of December 2014. We also found that facilities had varying levels of clinical time that was not used for patient care, regardless of whether they needed additional psychiatrists. VITA facilities could have better used an estimated 25 percent of psychiatrist FTE clinical time to see veterans during FY 2014, which equated to nearly $113.5 million in psychiatrists' pay. Over the next 5 years, this clinic time not used for patient care would equate to over $567 million if clinic management is not strengthened now.

Veterans' Access Needs Improvement

VHA did not effectively use psychiatrists in its efforts to improve veterans' access to psychiatric care. VHA significantly increased the number of psychiatrists providing outpatient clinical care since FY 2012, but did not show a corresponding increase in veterans receiving care from psychiatrists.

From FY 2012 through FY 2014, VHA increased the number of psychiatrist FTEs by about 226 outpatient clinical FTEs (nearly 15 percent). During the same period, the total number of veterans' outpatient encounters with psychiatrists increased about 10 percent, and the number of individual veterans who received outpatient care from a psychiatrist increased about 9 percent. As shown in the following figure, the nationwide rates of increase of veterans obtaining care from psychiatrists and their total encounters with psychiatrists, were not commensurate with the increase in FTEs allocated to provide that care.

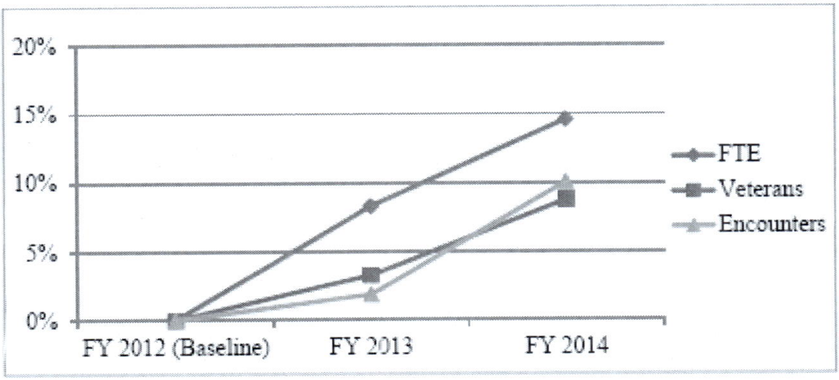

Source: OIG analysis of outpatient FTEs from VHA's Physician Productivity Cube and outpatient psychiatrist data obtained from VHA's Office of Productivity, Efficiency, and Staffing.

Figure 1. Percent Increase in Outpatient Psychiatrist FTEs, Individual Veterans, and Encounters From FY 2012 Through FY 2014.

Some individual facilities did not increase encounters from FY 2012 through FY 2014 even with their additional psychiatrist FTEs. For example, Minneapolis, MN, VA Medical Center (VAMC) increased FTEs by over 14 percent, but decreased encounters by over 21 percent. In contrast, Miami VAMC increased its psychiatrist clinical outpatient FTE by about 25 percent and increased encounters by just over 36 percent. Miami, FL, VAMC's Chief of Psychiatry and a lead program analyst actively monitored psychiatrists' workload and productivity data.

An OMHO official stated it was unknown what the appropriate increase in encounters should have been. He suggested that the addition of new staff might have curtailed psychiatrists' workload to a more manageable level.

As shown in Table 1, veterans nationwide received roughly the same frequency of encounters with psychiatrists in FY 2014 (3.56 encounters per veteran) as they did in FY 2012 (3.52 encounters per veteran), despite a nearly 15 percent increase in psychiatrist FTEs.

Table 1. Veterans Accessing Psychiatrists in VHA

Unit of Measure	FY 2012	FY 2014	Increase	Percent Change
Encounters	2,811,379	3,093,840	282,461	10.0%
Individual Veterans	799,181	869,018	69,837	8.7%
Frequency of Encounters	3.52	3.56	0.04	1.2%

Source: OIG analysis of outpatient psychiatrist data obtained from VHA's Office of Productivity, Efficiency, and Staffing

Note: Because of rounding, columns may not sum.

We determined that 59 of 129 facilities (over 45 percent) did not increase the average number of psychiatrist encounters per veteran from FY 2012 through FY 2014.[1] An OMHO official said that an improvement in the frequency of encounters would depend on several factors, including whether the facility gained additional patients. For example, if the number of individual patients at a facility increased by 10 percent, that facility may not be able to provide a corresponding increase in the veterans' frequency of encounters without an increase in psychiatrist FTEs. However, if VHA established a method for identifying staffing needs for psychiatrists at individual facilities, VHA would ensure that facilities with increased numbers of patients received additional FTEs.

No Uniform Staffing Approach

During a 2012 hiring initiative and throughout recent hiring efforts, VHA did not stress a specific need for psychiatrists and provided individual VISNs and facilities the latitude to determine their own staffing needs using their own methods. Two primary hiring efforts follow.

- During the 2012 hiring initiative, VHA did not implement a specific approach to distribute the 1,600 mental health clinicians, including psychiatrists. OMHO created a model that estimated the number of mental health staff each facility should add, but the model did not specify the type of clinicians those facilities needed. Thus, VHA did not define or plan for the number of psychiatrists that facilities needed.

- In 2014, despite established staffing goals for psychiatrists within mental health services, VHA continued to rely upon each VISN and its facilities to make staffing decisions because VHA believed the facilities were in the best position to address their unique veteran demand for mental health services.

2012 Hiring Initiative Did Not Focus on Psychiatrists

In 2012, at the request of several congressional leaders, OIG completed a review of veterans' access to mental health care. The 2012 report determined that one of VHA's greatest challenges in providing timely mental health care was its ability to hire and retain psychiatrists. On April 19, 2012, in response to congressional hearings over Congress's growing frustration to ensure veterans received timely access to mental health care, the former Secretary of Veterans Affairs announced VHA would hire approximately 1,600 mental health clinicians—including nurses, psychiatrists, psychologists, and social workers.

On April 25, 2012, the then-Chairman of the Senate Committee on Veterans' Affairs commended VA for the decision to hire additional mental health providers, but stated that VHA did not have a "reliable staffing model to determine where individuals were needed." In response, the former VHA Deputy Under Secretary for Health for Operations and Management stated that three VISNs were testing a staffing model. He testified that the model would provide a clear basis for assessing staffing for mental health services, and currently showed there were shortfalls at some sites nationally. In addition, he testified that psychiatrists were the most difficult mental health clinicians to recruit. He added during the hearing that:

> Decisions concerning staffing and programs were determined historically at the facility level to allow flexibility based on local resources and needs. However, as evidence accumulates, it is clear that sites can benefit from more central guidance on best practices in determining needed mental health staff.

In May 2012, VHA provided each VISN with facility-specific recommendations for the distribution of the additional clinical mental health FTEs. The recommendation identified the number of staff each facility should receive, but did not specify which types of mental health clinicians that facilities should hire. VHA determined the recommended hiring distribution by identifying facilities with lower rates of mental health clinician FTEs. Specifically, OMHO determined that each facility should have at least 7.72 mental health clinicians per 1,000 mental health patients.

During VHA's 2012 hiring initiative, VHA provided VISNs the latitude to hire other types of mental health clinicians or to move FTE allocations to a different facility if their ability to hire a certain clinician, such as a psychiatrist, within the period was difficult or unlikely. Then in June 2013, VA announced it had hired over 1,600 new mental health clinicians. However, based on information from VHA's Workforce Management and Consulting Office, VHA added only about 150 new outpatient psychiatrist FTEs through this initiative. This turned out to be an increase from the estimated 57 psychiatrists the former Secretary of Veterans Affairs testified to Congress in May 2012 that VHA planned to hire. The then-OMHO Director told us that VHA's goal was to ensure it hired 1,600 mental health clinicians and, in theory, would have approved hiring 1,600 social workers if that was what the VISNs stated they needed. She further stated that OMHO did not need to know how many psychiatrists VHA needed on a national level.

As of May 2013, after completion of the 2012 initiative to hire 1,600 additional mental health clinicians, OMHO determined that more than 60 facilities were still below what it determined to be a minimally acceptable mental health clinician staffing goal per facility—at least 7.72 mental health clinicians per 1,000 mental health patients. At that time, OMHO had not determined how many psychiatrists each facility needed. Thus, it did not know how many facilities still needed psychiatrists.

VHA Not Ensuring Facilities Meet Staffing Levels in 2014–2015 Hiring Plans

In 2014, despite established staffing ratios for psychiatrists within mental health services, VHA continued to rely upon each VISN and its facilities to make staffing decisions because VHA believed the facilities were in the best position to address their unique veteran demand for mental health services. On September 16, 2014, and again on December 29, 2014, VHA sent the VISNs a staffing model intended to drive the influx of hiring actions brought on in part by the Veterans Access, Choice, and Accountability Act of 2014. The staffing model established a minimum psychiatrist staffing level for facilities to be 1.22 outpatient psychiatrist FTEs per 1,000 individual mental health patients.

OMHO derived the 1.22 model based on the median level of psychiatrists at facilities nationwide. According to OMHO, staff-to-veteran ratios directly correlate with access to care.

However, OMHO did not require facilities to follow the estimated staffing model it provided. OMHO stated the model was used as guidance for the VISNs. It also stated it established the ratio in an effort to prevent VISNs and facilities from hiring easy-to-recruit, or less expensive mental health clinicians, in order to achieve the targeted FTE allocation. OMHO believed facilities that fell below the 1.22 ratio tended to be less efficient, because facilities need psychiatrists to make a number of important decisions that non-psychiatrists cannot legally or medically make. In December 2014, VHA's staffing model showed that 94 facilities were below this ratio.

Instead of using the staffing model to drive hiring decisions, VHA requested that VISNs and facilities provide budget and hiring plans based on the facilities' identified needs. VHA again allowed VISNs to move FTEs among their facilities, or to different care services, at the discretion of the VISN. According to OMHO, VISNs and facilities would make the decisions about actual numbers of hires, with input from VHA program offices.

VHA's estimate in December 2014 showed that 94 facilities needed nearly 335 psychiatrist FTEs to meet veteran demand. During January 2015, the VISNs revised VHA's December 2014 hiring plan. However, the VISNs requested only roughly 313 additional psychiatrist FTEs. While the VISNs' requested total was close to the total of what VHA estimated they needed, the VISNs' request reallocated psychiatrist FTEs to different facilities. For example, OMHO's model suggested that one facility needed 24 additional psychiatrist FTEs, but the VISN requested only 12 psychiatrists for that facility.

If facilities hire psychiatrist FTEs according to the VISNs' January 2015 estimated staffing plans, 62 facilities would remain understaffed with psychiatrists based on what OMHO determined they needed to meet veteran demand. This would result in a similar outcome to the 2012 hiring initiative, when OMHO determined that more than 60 facilities remained below minimum staffing level for mental health clinicians.

VHA lacked an effective method for establishing psychiatrist staffing needs at individual facilities. While VA has established staffing models within mental health services, it has not ensured facilities followed the staffing ratios. VHA should ensure VISNs and facilities incorporate OMHO's staffing model to determine the appropriate number of psychiatrists needed for outpatient care and work together to attain appropriate staffing levels or identify alternative options to meet veteran demand for psychiatrists. This would improve veterans' access to care through effective placement of resources.

Clinic Management Practices Allowed for Unused Capacity

VHA clinic management practices resulted in unused capacity of its psychiatrists. We determined that the facilities we visited did not use consistent and effective standards for how many veterans their psychiatrists could care for or for their psychiatrists' time available for direct patient care. Facilities varied in their own expectations of such practices, which resulted in different levels of access. As a result of OIG's *Audit of VHA's Physician Staffing Levels for Specialty Care Services* and previous VHA studies, VHA recently implemented productivity measures. However, VHA should reassess its established productivity target.

Veterans per Psychiatrist

VHA did not have standards for the appropriate number of veterans its psychiatrists could care for. During FY 2014, the average number of unique veterans that a psychiatrist FTE provided care to during the year ranged from 311 veterans at one facility to 906 veterans at another facility. Facilities with high veteran-to-psychiatrist ratios generally have less opportunity to provide additional appointments to existing or new patients. As shown in Table 2, in FY 2014, the average number of psychiatrist patients per psychiatrist FTEs during a 1-year period was 502 unique veterans.

An OMHO official confirmed that VHA did not have an internal measure or benchmark for the number of patients per psychiatrist. Therefore, facilities determined their own expectations of how many veterans their psychiatrists could care for, which resulted in different ranges of access. Three examples follow.

Example 1

Temple, TX, VAMC's average was 669 patients per psychiatrist during FY 2014, and veterans received an average of just over 2.7 encounters with psychiatrists during the year. The Chief of Mental Health said on average an ideal maximum caseload for a psychiatrist would be approximately 800 veterans per psychiatrist.

Table 2. Average Number of Psychiatrist Patients per Psychiatrist FTE

VA Facility	FY 2012	FY 2014
Lowest VA Facility	306	311
San Francisco	306	316
New York Harbor	420	400
Miami	489	449
National Average	529	502
Dublin	711	545
Chillicothe	648	634
Temple	729	669
Highest VA Facility	1,114	906

Source: OIG analysis of VHA's Physician Productivity Cube and outpatient psychiatrist data obtained from VHA's Office of Productivity, Efficiency, and Staffing.

Example 2

New York Harbor Healthcare System's average was 400 patients per psychiatrist during FY 2014, and veterans received an average of 5.3 encounters with psychiatrists during the year. The Chief of Mental Health said their ratios should be about 500 veterans per psychiatrist.

Example 3

VA Texas Valley Coastal Bend Health Care System had the nation's highest ratio of approximately 906 patients per psychiatrist, and veterans received only about 2 encounters per year with psychiatrists.

Use of Clinical Time for Patient Care

On average, a psychiatrist clinical FTE scheduled appointments with veterans only for an estimated 22.4 hours per week during FY 2014. The six facilities we visited had varied expectations on the number of hours each psychiatrist should spend on clinical time, ranging from 25 to 32.5 hours during a 40-hour week. In 2014, OMHO presented analysis to VHA leadership regarding the percentage of clinical time that is "bookable." OMHO suggested that about 78 percent of clinicians' worked clinical hours per year are bookable and should be spent in generating encounters. This equates to 31.2 hours in a 40-hour week for a clinical FTE. OMHO suggested clinicians would use their remaining working clinical time for other patient care-related activities, such as team meetings, documentation, and phone calls.

Table 3 depicts the average number of hours a psychiatrist FTE used to complete encounters with veterans during a week, assuming 31.2 hours per week should be spent in encounters with veterans. We considered missed opportunities, such as patient no-shows, as scheduled time, and counted that time as used even though a veteran did not receive an encounter.[2] On average, a psychiatrist clinical FTE scheduled only 22.4 out of 31.2 potential hours per week during FY 2014, leaving over 8.8 hours unscheduled.

Table 3. Psychiatrist FTEs' Use of Patient Care Time per Week

VA Facility	Total Scheduled Hours— Out of 31.2 Potential Hours	Potential Hours Remaining to Schedule Veterans
New York Harbor	29.1	2.1
Miami	27.2	4.0
Temple	24.6	6.6
Chillicothe	24.3	6.9
National Average	22.4	8.8
Dublin	19.6	11.6
San Francisco	19.0	12.2

Source: OIG analysis of outpatient psychiatrists' patient care time and completed encounters obtained from VHA's Office of Productivity, Efficiency, and Staffing.

VA facilities could have used the remaining clinical time to complete additional outpatient appointments for veterans. In total, we estimated VA facilities did not use about 706,000 hours of patient care time to generate encounters with veterans. VITA facilities could have better used an estimated 25 percent (706,000 hours / 2.88 million potential hours) of psychiatrist FTE clinical time to see veterans during FY 2014, which equated to nearly $113.5 million in psychiatrists' pay. Over the next 5 years, that clinical time not used for patient care will equate to over $567 million if clinic management is not strengthened.

Improving the use of patient care hours from 22.4 hours to 31.2 hours would provide more appointments to those veterans seeking mental health care. VITA should develop clinic management business rules to ensure facilities consistently monitor the use of clinical time and number of veterans per psychiatrist, in conjunction with monitoring psychiatrists' productivity. Improved clinic management practices across VITA would assist facilities in efficiently using psychiatrists in their outpatient mental health clinics.

Productivity

VITA should reassess its established productivity measure. During FY 2014, the average outpatient psychiatrist FTE exceeded the target by over 22 percent. VITA Directive 1161, *Productivity and Staffing In Outpatient Clinical Encounters for Mental Health Providers* (June 7, 2013), states psychiatrists should strive for a yearly productivity target above 2,574 Relative Value Units (RVUs), though VITA considers productivity between 2,317 and 2,831 RVUs as meeting the standard.

An RVU is a measure of the complexity and time required to perform a professional service. For purposes of the productivity measurement, only the work component of the RVU value is used. The 2,574 RVU target is adjusted based on the individual's leave during the period and time allotted for direct patient care. Managers can use this to evaluate a psychiatrist's productivity.

Although psychiatrists did not use all of their clinic time to schedule and complete encounters with veterans, VITA's productivity measure indicated generally high psychiatrist productivity. VITA's productivity target for psychiatrists is based on the median RVU rate during FY 2011.

As shown in Table 4, nationwide, the average outpatient psychiatrist FTE exceeded the 2,574 target by over 22 percent.

Table 4. Outpatient Psychiatrist Productivity During FY 2014

VA Facility	Average RVUs per FTE	Difference From VHA Target
Lowest VA Facility	1,017	(60.5%)
Chillicothe	3,112	20.9%
National Average	3,145	22.2%
New York Harbor	3,268	27.0%
Dublin	3,365	30.7%
San Francisco	3,409	32.4%
Temple	4,005	55.6%
Miami	4,268	65.8%
Highest VA Facility	5,417	110.4%

Source: OIG analysis of VHA's Physician Productivity Cube and outpatient psychiatrist data obtained from VHA's Office of Productivity, Efficiency, and Staffing.

In total, 106 of 140 facilities (76 percent) exceeded VHA's psychiatrist productivity target in FY 2014. Of those, 90 facilities exceeded the target by more than 10 percent during FY 2014. VHA Directive 1161 states that significantly high productivity numbers might suggest a need to reassign staff. In addition, productivity numbers significantly higher or lower than the target might reflect improper coding, and service chiefs are encouraged to monitor for compliance with national coding guidelines.

Nearly two-thirds of VHA facilities exceeded the VHA psychiatrist productivity target by more than 10 percent during FY 2014. The national average exceeded the target by over 22 percent. VHA attributed some of the increase in RVUs to a 2013 change in current procedure terminology (CPT) code values, which included an increase in the value of some CPT codes that psychiatrists use. However, VHA did not make a corresponding increase to VHA's RVU target. VHA should reassess the appropriateness of its RVU target for psychiatrists.

Procedure Coding

Inconsistent and inappropriate procedure coding by psychiatrists lessened the reliability of their total RVUs. VHA's productivity measure is dependent on psychiatrists to accurately record workload using CPT codes. Psychiatrists record CPT codes for encounters they complete with veterans to record a work value for work performed. Each CPT code has a work value assigned called an RVU, which makes up the productivity measure. However, we determined that:

- Psychiatrists inconsistently applied procedural coding.
- Psychiatrists inappropriately recorded duplicate procedure codes on single encounters.

Inconsistent Procedure Coding

The six sampled facilities used different CPT codes for similar patient encounters. It was reasonable to expect variances based on each facility's veteran demographics and the complexity of care provided. However, the following is an example of psychiatrists of different facilities using different CPT codes for similar types of encounters.

Example 4

VHA psychiatrists used CPT codes 99211 and 99215 to record an outpatient encounter with an established patient. CPT code 99211 represents a less-complex encounter and has a value of 0.18 RVUs. CPT code 99215 represents a more complex encounter and has a value of 2.11 RVUs. Nationally, the more complex CPT code 99215 accounted for less than 2 percent of CPT codes used by outpatient psychiatrists during FY 2014. At the Dublin, GA, VAMC, CPT code 99215 accounted for about 27 percent of all CPT codes recorded by outpatient psychiatrists during FY 2014.

Figure 2 depicts the average RVUs per clinical outpatient psychiatrist FTE for the six sampled facilities, as well as the national average. As shown in the figure, the average RVU value recorded by psychiatrists at New York Harbor Healthcare System (1a complexity facility) was lower per encounter than the national average during FY 2014. In contrast, the Dublin, Temple, and San Francisco VAMCs (3, 1b, and 1a complexity, respectively) recorded higher RVU values than the national average.

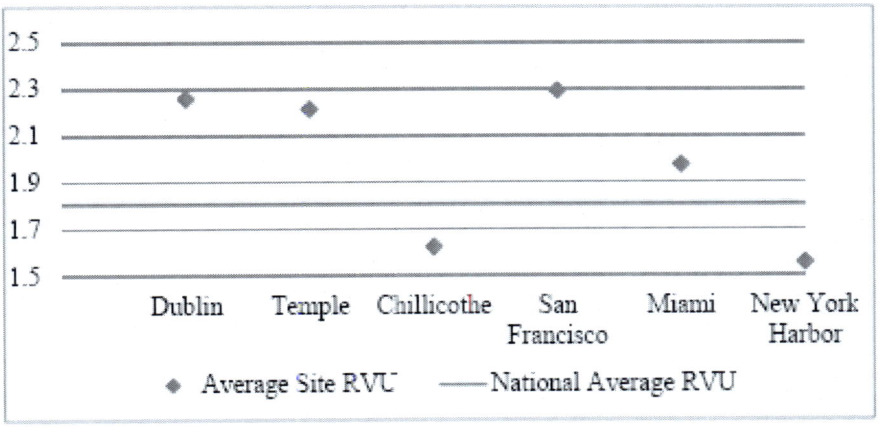

Source: OIG analysis of VHA's Physician Productivity Cube and outpatient psychiatrist data obtained from VHA's Office of Productivity, Efficiency, and Staffing.

Figure 2. Average Psychiatrist RVU per Encounter During FY 2014.

OMHO acknowledged that there are inconsistencies in coding in VHA, and psychiatrists received minimal training for coding.

Duplicate Procedure Coding

Psychiatrists at Dublin VAMC and Chillicothe, OH, VAMC inappropriately recorded duplicate CPT codes on single encounters. Dublin VAMC inappropriately recorded 953 duplicate CPT codes on 941 outpatient encounters by applying the same CPT code multiple times to each encounter during FY 2013. Chillicothe VAMC inappropriately recorded 645 duplicate CPT codes on 215 encounters for psychiatric evaluations during FY 2012. This resulted in overstated RVUs by over 12 percent and nearly 9 percent, respectively, during that time.

According to OMHO and facility staff, psychiatrists did not have routine CPT training. In addition, OMHO officials said they generally only reviewed CPT codes for quality assurance in instances in which third party insurance was used for the encounter. To ensure accurate procedure coding and reliable productivity values, VHA should develop a mechanism to monitor the variance in which psychiatrists code encounters, and determine appropriate coding guidance and training to ensure consistency. This would improve VHA's ability to use RVU data to evaluate productivity and make informed staffing decisions.

Conclusion

VHA needs to take action to establish effective clinic management practices and to identify specific psychiatrist staffing needs at individual facilities. While VHA significantly increased the number of psychiatrists providing outpatient clinical care, veterans' access to those psychiatrists can still improve. VHA identified in December 2014 that 94 facilities needed 335 psychiatrist FTEs to meet known veteran demand. In addition, we determined that facilities nationwide had an estimated 25 percent of psychiatrist FTE clinical time during FY 2014 that they could have used to complete additional outpatient encounters with veterans. By identifying the appropriate number of psychiatrists that facilities need, and implementing effective clinic management business rules, VHA could optimally place and use psychiatrists. This would improve access for veterans currently receiving psychiatrists' care, as well as future, unmet veteran demand.

RECOMMENDATIONS

1. We recommended the Under Secretary for Health ensure Veteran Integrated Service Networks and medical facilities incorporate the Office of Mental Health Operations staffing model to determine the appropriate number of psychiatrists needed for outpatient care, and work with those facilities to attain appropriate staffing levels or identify alternative options to meet veteran demand for psychiatrists.

2. We recommended the Under Secretary for Health develop clinic management business rules to ensure facilities consistently monitor the use of clinical time and number of veterans per psychiatrist, in conjunction with monitoring psychiatrists' productivity.
3. We recommended the Under Secretary for Health reassess the appropriateness of the Veterans Health Administration's productivity target for psychiatrists.
4. We recommended the Under Secretary for Health develop a mechanism to monitor the variance in which psychiatrists code encounters and determine appropriate coding guidance and training to ensure consistency.

Agency Comments

The Under Secretary for Health concurred with our findings and recommendations and stated that VHA would implement Recommendations 1–3 by September 2016, and that VHA had already implemented Recommendation 4. The Under Secretary for Health's entire verbatim response is located in Appendix C.

OIG Response

The Under Secretary for Health's planned corrective actions are acceptable. We will monitor VHA's progress and follow up on the implementation of our recommendations until all proposed actions are completed. We consider Recommendation 4 closed based on VHA's actions and planned ongoing guidance, training, and monitoring by VA Central Office and local supervisors.

APPENDIX A. SCOPE AND METHODOLOGY

Audit Scope

We conducted our audit work from December 2013 through July 2015. The audit focused on veterans' access to outpatient psychiatrists in mental health care. This audit was delayed for several months as a result of the OIG's efforts to address patient wait time allegations at the Phoenix VA Health Care System and at VA health care facilities nationwide.

VHA defines outpatient care as encounters between veterans and providers within the VA health care system that take place without an inpatient stay. We reviewed physicians that VHA's Office of Productivity, Efficiency, and Staffing (OPES) identified under the specialty care service of psychiatry. We also reviewed the encounters completed by those psychiatrists. An encounter is a professional contact between a patient and a practitioner vested with responsibility for diagnosing, evaluating, and treating the patient's condition. We did not include encounter data that OPES identified as duplicates, phantom encounters (appointments that were placeholders but no care was actually provided), or encounters for lab work. We also did not include non-VA paid physicians or their encounters.

We analyzed VHA data of outpatient psychiatrist clinical FTEs, psychiatrists' encounters, CPT codes, veteran demand, psychiatrist pay, and productivity during FYs 2012, 2013, and 2014. We also reviewed VHA's hiring efforts and clinic management practices over psychiatrists at six randomly sampled VA medical facilities.

This audit did not assess the quality of care psychiatrists or mental health clinics provided to veterans. Veterans receive VA mental health care from many different types of mental health clinicians other than psychiatrists, including psychologists, social workers, nurse practitioners, and others. According to VA testimony from November 2011, psychiatrists in VA typically provide medication management, and veterans see a psychologist, social worker, or other licensed mental health provider for psychotherapy. However, psychiatrists can also provide psychotherapy if it is determined that it is clinically indicated. VA further stated that there are no national VA policies in place that restrict psychiatrists from providing any service that they determine is clinically indicated, as long as it is within their scope of practice.

Methodology

The audit focused on VHA's hiring efforts and clinic management practices in regards to access to outpatient psychiatrists.

To address our audit objective, we performed the following actions.

- Conducted site visits to VA facilities in Chillicothe, OH; Dublin, GA; Miami, FL; New York Harbor, NY; San Francisco, CA; and Temple, TX

- Interviewed VHA's OMHO officials, VHA's Workforce Management and Consulting officials, facility chiefs of staff, facility mental health service chiefs, staff psychiatrists, human resources staff, administrative officers, and billing and coding staff
- Analyzed VHA mental health hiring initiative plans and estimated staffing needs
- Obtained and analyzed data from VHA's OPES, and VHA Support Service Center's Physician Productivity Cube and Mental Health Cube

Although VHA collects and reports mental health wait time data, we did not include wait time data in this audit. OIG and VHA have determined over recent years that VHA's wait time data are unreliable. The inaccuracies in the data hinder the usability of information; therefore, we did not rely on such data in this report.

Psychiatrists' Pay

We identified the average annual cost for a psychiatrist FTE using the VHA Support Service Center Mental Health Cube. We determined the average pay and benefits of an outpatient psychiatrist FTE was $260,752 during FY 2014. We verified the Mental Health Cube pay data with information identified in VA's Personnel and Accounting Integrated Data.

Psychiatrists' Time

We analyzed psychiatrists' clinic time based on encounter data and individual veteran data obtained from OPES, and clinical outpatient psychiatrist FTE from the Physician Productivity Cube.

We compared the potential clinical time with scheduled and completed encounters, per clinical FTE, with the number of actual completed encounters. We determined that established patient encounters are generally 30 minutes, and new patient encounters are generally 1 hour. Based on the number of unique veterans who received care in FY 2014, but did not receive care in FY 2013, we estimated the total number of potential encounters a clinical outpatient psychiatrist FTE could have completed, and then we compared that with the number of actual completed encounters during FY 2014.

We evaluated clinic time by calculating the additional time clinical outpatient psychiatrist FTEs could have used to complete encounters, based on 31.2 potential hours per week. The average weekly rate was based on all outpatient encounters that psychiatrists completed during FY 2014, and reflected the average missed opportunity rate.

Fraud Assessment

The audit team assessed the risk that fraud, violations of legal and regulatory requirements, and abuse could occur during this audit. The audit team exercised due diligence in staying alert to any fraud indicators. We did not identify any instances of fraud during this audit.

Data Reliability

We relied on computer-processed data obtained from OPES, as well as data obtained from the VHA Support Service Center Physician Productivity Cube and Mental Health Cube. We assessed the reliability of the data obtained from OPES and the Physician Productivity Cube by comparing 30 randomly selected encounter records with those veterans' individual medical records. We tested these data to determine reliability of overall encounters, number of individual veterans, and number of outpatient FTEs. We also obtained information from the Physician Productivity Cube system owner, reviewed systems documentation, and reviewed the data to identify obvious errors in accuracy and completeness to ensure that the Physician Productivity Cube had the most complete data available regarding outpatient psychiatrist RVUs. Based on these tests, we concluded the data were sufficiently reliable to meet the objective of the audit.

We assessed the reliability of psychiatrist pay from the VHA Support Service Center Mental Health Cube by comparing it with data collected from VA's Personnel and Accounting Integrated Data. We determined that the average pay for a psychiatrist FTE identified in the two sources were different by just over 1 percent. We then compared the sums of facility specific gross pay for psychiatrists from VA's Personnel and Accounting Integrated Data with the facility-supplied data. We determined the average gross pay identified in the two sources were different by less than 3 percent. Based on these tests, we concluded the average psychiatrist pay identified in the Mental Health Cube was sufficiently reliable for the purposes of this audit.

Government Standards

Our assessment of internal controls focused on those controls relating to our audit objectives. We conducted this performance audit in accordance with generally accepted government auditing standards. These standards require that we plan and perform the audit to obtain sufficient, appropriate evidence to provide a reasonable basis for our findings and conclusions based on our audit objective. We believe that the evidence obtained provides a reasonable basis for our findings and conclusions based on our audit objective.

APPENDIX B. POTENTIAL MONETARY BENEFITS IN ACCORDANCE WITH INSPECTOR GENERAL ACT AMENDMENTS

Recommendation	Explanation of Benefits	Better Use of Funds	Questioned Costs
2	VA facilities could have better used an estimated 25 percent of psychiatrist FTE clinic time to see veterans during FY 2014. This time equated to nearly $113.5 million in psychiatrists' pay in FY 2014; it could equal $567 million over the next 5 years.	$567,000,000	$0
	Total $567,000,000		*$0*

Potential Monetary Benefit Calculation

We determined the estimated potential monetary benefits using the following analysis and assumptions.

- According to OMHO, about 78 percent of clinicians' worked clinic hours are "bookable" and should be spent in generating encounters (2,080 total hours x 78 percent = 1,622 patient care hours per clinical FTE per year).
- We identified approximately 2.88 million total hours (1,776 clinical FTEs x 1,622 patient care hours per year = 2.88 million hours).

- We determined that psychiatrists did not use more than 706,000 hours to complete encounters, which equated to about 25 percent of patient care time (706,000 hours / 2.88 million hours = 24.5 percent).
- The clinical time not used for patient care during FY 2014 equated to 435 psychiatrist FTEs (1,776 clinical FTEs x 24.5 percent = 435.18 clinical FTEs not used for patient care).
- We determined the average pay and benefits of a psychiatrist FTE was $260,752 during FY 2014, which equated to nearly $113.5 million in clinical time not used for patient care ($260,752 x 435.18 clinical FTEs = $113.5 million).

This equates to better use of funds totaling over $567 million over the next 5 years if clinic management is not strengthened.

APPENDIX C UNDER SECRETARY FOR HEALTH COMMENTS

Department of Veterans Affairs **Memorandum**

Date: July 28, 2015

From: Under Secretary for Health (10)

Subj: Office of Inspector General (OIG) Draft Report: Audit of VHA's Efforts to Improve Veterans' Access to Outpatient Psychiatrists (7620108)

To: Assistant Inspector General for Audits and Evaluations (52)

1. Thank you for the opportunity to review the OIG draft report of the Audit of VHA's Efforts to Improve Veterans' Access to Outpatient Psychiatrists.
2. I concur with the findings and recommendations in the draft report and provide comments in response to recommendation 1-4.
3. Please direct questions or concerns regarding the content of this memorandum to Karen Rasmussen, M.D., Director, Management Review Service (10AR) at VHA10ARMRS2@va.gov.

David J. Shulkin, M.D.

Attachment

VETERANS HEALTH ADMINISTRATION (VHA) ACTION PLAN OFFICE OF INSPECTOR GENERAL'S (OIG) DRAFT REPORT AUDIT OF VHA'S EFFORTS TO IMPROVE VETERANS' ACCESS TO OUTPATIENT PSYCHIATRISTS

Date of Draft Report: July 2, 2015

Recommendations/ Actions	Status	Target Completion Date

Recommendation 1. We recommended the Under Secretary for Health ensure Veteran Integrated Service Networks and facilities incorporate the Office of Mental Health Operations staffing model to determine the appropriate number of psychiatrists needed for outpatient care, and work with those facilities to attain appropriate staffing levels or identify alternative options to meet veteran demand for psychiatrists.

Comments: Concur

Importantly, the psychiatry staffing benchmark is not a VHA policy requirement. VHA agrees that each Veterans Integrated Service Network (VISN) and facility should use the current benchmark: 1.22 psychiatrist full-time employee equivalent (FTEE) per 1,000 outpatient mental health (MH) service-using Veterans. Facilities should consider this when developing their staffing plans for MH services.

The Office of Mental Health Operations (OMHO) recently implemented a dashboard that displays the status of the psychiatry staffing benchmark for each facility and is scheduling recurring MH management conversations with VISN clinical leaders to review that information.

OMHO supports the responsibilities of VISNs and facilities for attaining and maintaining sufficient psychiatry staffing, including utilizing "alternative options" such as delivery of care via telemental health from other sites or the community, non-VA mechanisms such as CHOICE, contract, or fee basis, and/or delivery of care as appropriate via advanced practice nurses, physician assistants, and/or clinically-trained pharmacists. Alternative options are useful in sites where the available professional population in the area is very small and recruiting is difficult. Additionally, VISN and facility leaders are encouraged to fully utilize available incentive strategies such as the Education Debt Repayment Program (including the recently authorized education debt repayment provisions of the Clay Hunt Act), geographic pay and scarce specialty pay. Finally, because retention of psychiatrists is generally more effective and less costly than recruitment of new psychiatrists, it is important that VISN and facility leaders ensure that salaries for currently employed VA psychiatrists are commensurate to salaries offered to new recruits.

To complete this action, VHA will:

1. Provide documentation that each VISN has submitted a plan to OMHO for psychiatric staffing by the end of fiscal year (FY) 2016, quarter 1. The plan must include the targeted number of FTEE psychiatrists per 1,000 outpatient MH service-using Veterans; an explanation of negative variance from the benchmark; recruiting and retention approaches; barriers to achieving the target; and alternative approaches to provide the services required to meet Veteran demand.
2. Monitor progress on hiring and vacancies as well as the staffing ratio in conjunction with Workforce Management and review this regularly with VISN MH and clinical leadership.

Status in process

Target Completion Date
September 30, 2016

Recommendation 2. We recommended the Under Secretary for Health develop clinic management business rules to ensure facilities consistently monitor the use of clinical time and number of veterans per psychiatrist, in conjunction with monitoring psychiatrists' productivity.

Comments: Concur

VHA supports a very critical process of setting individualized productivity targets for psychiatrists. VHA also specifies productivity benchmarks for the discipline as a whole. This process is aimed at optimizing access to and quality of care for Veterans in psychiatric care. However, VHA does not support the use of business rules for defining exact hours of face-to-face clinical care and numbers of patients served for all psychiatrists as this is counterproductive in an environment in which different psychiatrists with different patient populations work in very different, but appropriate, manners.

VHA has implemented a policy regarding productivity of MH providers, including psychiatrists, in VHA Directive 1161, Productivity and Staffing in Outpatient Clinical Encounters for Mental Health Providers. That directive provides policy on outpatient provider productivity based on outpatient clinical encounters for all psychiatrists and psychologists, as well as for those advanced practice nurses, social workers, and physician assistants who work in mental health settings. OMHO has provided support for implementation of the directive in a variety of ways, including: Mental Health Business Operations monthly national calls, facilitation of productivity management training sessions for individual sites and VISNs, reviews of discipline productivity in quarterly MH management conversations between OMHO and VISN leadership, OMHO site visits, and through individual reviews with facility and VISN leaders.

Recently, each facility leadership team received a memo from VA Central Office (VACO) asking for verification that each MH provider (as required by the productivity directive) has an established individualized productivity target. While OMHO does not require a fixed percentage of hours spent in direct patient contact (of hours mapped to clinical care), teaching on how to use the productivity tools suggests that 70-80 percent of that time be in direct contact with Veterans for those assigned to general mental health clinical settings full-time.

The benchmark of 1.22 FTEE psychiatrists per 1,000 outpatient MH service-using Veterans suggests that a site would have roughly 820 Veterans per psychiatrist FTEE. However, some of these Veterans engaged in MH care would not require care from a psychiatrist so the number of patients treated on a single psychiatrist's panel would almost always be less than 820. The number of Veterans a single psychiatrist can safely and effectively manage varies widely based on type of mental disorder. For example, Veterans with schizophrenia or dementia often require more time than those with depression. Veterans with more severe mental disorders, new diagnoses and those with chronic conditions may require more time than those with unstable, severe conditions. Similarly, the structure of the clinical team may affect psychiatrist work-load as some work alone and others work with additional therapists, case managers and nurses. Thus, the number of Veterans per psychiatrist is a local decision made by taking into account many variables. OMHO agrees that psychiatrist panel size should be monitored during the regular local review of productivity with each provider.

To complete this action plan, VHA will:

1. Verify that all facilities have implemented individual productivity targets for psychiatrists.
2. Monitor VISNs' and facilities' psychiatric productivity measures as well as work Relative Value Units (wRVU)/encounter metric through the OMHO dashboard.
3. Address outliers on these measures with VISN leadership regularly in the MH management conversations.
4. Issue guidance regarding appropriate percentages of time mapped for psychiatric clinical activity to be spent in face-to-face care of Veterans. This guidance will require a discussion of wRVUs, encounters, labor mapping of clinical hours, and unique Veterans served as well as the overall productivity measure during each productivity review with a psychiatrist.
5. Offer continued education, support and training provided to VISN and facility leadership as needed.

Status	Target Completion Date
In process	September 30, 2016

Recommendation 3. We recommended the Under Secretary for Health reassess the appropriateness of the Veterans Health Administration's productivity target for psychiatrists.

Comments: Concur

As noted in the productivity directive, VHA will review and readjust targets for productivity for each type of provider covered by the directive. Due to the large-scale change in current procedural codes (CPT) for psychiatrists that occurred during 2013, VHA deferred readjusting psychiatrists' productivity targets until there was a stable year of activity. OMHO analysts and leadership will examine the distribution of wRVUs by psychiatrist FTEE and the relationship of this metric to Veteran satisfaction with access to providers to determine an appropriate target that best serves cost-efficiency and access.

To complete this action, VHA will provide documentation of OMHO findings and/or decisions regarding changes to psychiatric productivity targets.

Status	Target Completion Date
In process	September 30, 2016

Recommendation 4. We recommended the Under Secretary for Health develop a mechanism to monitor the variance in which psychiatrists code encounters, and determine appropriate coding guidance and training to ensure consistency.

Comments: Concur

VHA agrees that a mechanism for coding psychiatric services that is reliable across psychiatrists and sites is important. To that end, on July 10, 2015, OMHO hosted a National business operations call devoted to this training on this task. OMHO and Mental Health Services staff from the Office of Patient Care Services combined to provide guidance on workload capture for mental health providers through its mental health coding guides.

This information is readily available to all VA psychiatrists and their leadership on National Sharepoints and has been presented on national training calls previously. OMHO will have ongoing calls regarding coding and workload capture throughout the year. OMHO analysts will shortly be able to identify differences in patterns of CPT code use across facilities and will be able to generate reports regarding outliers. Through use of the Office of Productivity, Efficiency, and Staffing physician productivity tool for psychiatrists, each facility MH chief or Associate Chief of Staff can review the array of CPT codes used by psychiatrists they supervise. This review may be used to intervene with psychiatrists to decrease variability and increase reliability of coding. Some variance is appropriate and expected as some psychiatrists have quite different practice patterns than others. For example, a psychiatrist involved in opiate agonist treatment might have large numbers of brief appointments whereas a psychiatrist providing geropsychiatric services might have longer appointments. Thus, guidance, training, and monitoring from VACO combined with investigations by local supervisors should improve consistency as recommended.

Status	Target Completion Date
Completed	July 2015

INDEX

A

B

C

L

M

N

O